Can Liberal States Accommodate Indigenous Peoples?

Political Theory Today series

Duncan Ivison

———————

Can Liberal States Accommodate Indigenous Peoples?

polity

The right of Duncan Ivison to be identified as Author of this Work has been asserted in accordance with the UK Copyright, Designs and Patents Act 1988.

First published in 2020 by Polity Press

Polity Press
65 Bridge Street
Cambridge CB2 1UR, UK

Polity Press
101 Station Landing
Suite 300
Medford, MA 02155, USA

ISBN-13: 978-1-5095-3297-1
ISBN-13: 978-1-5095-3298-8 (pb)

A catalogue record for this book is available from the British Library.

Typeset in 11 on 15pt Sabon
by Fakenham Prepress Solutions, Fakenham, Norfolk NR21 8NL
Printed and bound in the UK by TJ International Limited

The publisher has used its best endeavours to ensure that the URLs for external websites referred to in this book are correct and active at the time of going to press. However, the publisher has no responsibility for the websites and can make no guarantee that a site will remain live or that the content is or will remain appropriate.

Every effort has been made to trace all copyright holders, but if any have been overlooked the publisher will be pleased to include any necessary credits in any subsequent reprint or edition.

For further information on Polity, visit our website: politybooks.com

Contents

Acknowledgements

I am deeply grateful for help, advice and inspiration from Sam Balaton-Chrimes, John Borrows, Danielle Celermajer, Simone Chambers, Glen Coulthard, Megan Davis, Mick Dodson, Andrew Fitzmaurice, Rainer Forst, Moira Gatens, Kirsty Gover, Stan Grant, Matthew Joseph, Jacob Levy, Lynn Meskell, Paul Patton, Noel Pearson, Audra Simpson, Quentin Skinner, Charles Taylor, Dale Turner, James Tully, Jeremy Webber and Melissa Williams. Three anonymous readers provided wise and encouraging comments on the penultimate draft, as did George Owers, who has also been a supportive editor. None should be held responsible for the errors and infelicities that remain.

I owe a debt of gratitude of a different order to Diana, Hamish and Isobel, for their continuous love and support.

Acknowledgements

This book is dedicated to the memory of my father – a quintessential liberal – who died shortly before I began writing it, but who nevertheless remained with me throughout.

Chapters 3 and 4 contain heavily revised material first published in 'The Logic of Aboriginal Rights', *Ethnicities* 3 (3) (2003): 321–44; and 'Pluralising Political Legitimacy', *Postcolonial Studies* 20 (1) (2017): 118–30.

Preface: Uluṟu

If you look at a map of Australia and search for Uluṟu, it appears to be almost at the centre of the country. It's located in the Central Desert region, 335 kilometres from Alice Springs. The name refers to the land of the Aṉangu, the traditional owners. Whether or not it *is* at the geographical heart of Australia – rather wonderfully, the Australian government's Geosciences division suggests there is no such thing[1] – the massive sandstone formation, standing almost 350 metres high, with a circumference of more than 9 kilometres, looms large in the geographical, spiritual and metaphysical landscape of both the Central Desert peoples and Australia. Uluṟu's history, in so many ways, encapsulates the struggles, hopes, fears, narrow-mindedness and generosity of Aboriginal and European relations over two centuries on this continent.

For the Anangu, the landscape, including Uluru, was created by their ancestral beings at the beginning of time; a connection that entails an unending responsibility to protect and care for those lands. For Europeans, Uluru was originally 'Ayers Rock', named by the British surveyor William Gosse in 1873 for his boss, the Chief Secretary of South Australia, Sir Henry Ayers. Throughout much of the twentieth century, Ayers Rock became an iconic tourist destination for Australian and international visitors. But it was also a place of struggle. In 1985, after a wave of strikes, protests and an insurgent land rights movement, the title to the land was finally returned to the Anangu. The park is now jointly managed by them and Parks Australia as Uluru-Kata Tjuta National Park.

In May 2017, Uluru played host to another significant moment in Australian history: the First Nations National Constitutional Convention. This meeting was the culmination of work begun by the Referendum Council, established in 2015, charged with advising on the best means for delivering recognition of Aboriginal and Torres Strait Islander peoples in Australia's constitution. As part of its work, the Council created a series of innovative 'First Nation Regional Dialogues' across Australia which prepared the groundwork for the Constitutional Convention, held at the foot of Uluru. What emerged from that meeting was a remarkable political declaration: the 'Uluru Statement from the Heart'. The allusion in the title is rich and powerful: a statement 'from the heart', declared at the metaphysical heart of Anangu country, aimed at the hearts of all Australians, attempting to cut to the heart of issues left unresolved for too long since European settlement. It begins thus:

> Our Aboriginal and Torres Strait Islander tribes were the first sovereign Nations of the Australian continent and its adjacent islands, and possessed it under our own laws and customs. ... With substantive constitutional change and structural reform, we believe this ancient sovereignty can shine through as a fuller expression of Australia's nationhood.

It continues:

> Proportionally, we are the most incarcerated people on the planet. We are not an innately criminal people. Our children are alienated from their families at unprecedented rates. This cannot be because we have no love for them. And our youth languish in detention in obscene numbers. They should be our hope for the future.
>
> These dimensions of our crisis tell plainly the structural nature of our problem. This is the torment of our powerlessness.

We seek constitutional reforms to empower our people and take a rightful place in our own country. When we have power over our destiny our children will flourish. They will walk in two worlds and their culture will be a gift to their country.

Three major recommendations emerged from the Convention and the 'Statement from the Heart'. The first was that a referendum should be held to enshrine a First Nations 'Voice' to Parliament. This would be a representative body of First Nations traditional owners to advise Parliament on policy affecting Aboriginal and Torres Strait Islander people. It would be a first step to addressing the 'torment of our powerlessness'. Further discussions would be needed to define exactly what kind of representative body it would be, but the constitutional guarantee of its existence was critical. Previous advisory bodies have been created but then dismissed at the whim of governments. At the same time, the Council made clear it was not intended to have a veto over legislation. It would be a political mechanism for enhancing dialogue and improving the lives of Indigenous peoples.

The second and third recommendations were extra-constitutional in nature. The Council recommended that a 'Declaration of Recognition' be enacted by legislation passed by all Australian parliaments, bringing together the three parts of the 'Australian story': 'our ancient First Peoples' heritage and culture, our British institutions, and our multicultural unity'. And finally, it recommends that a 'Makarrata Commission' be established; the 'culmination of our agenda', as the Statement puts it. Makarrata is a Yolngu word taken from a dispute resolution ceremony from the Gumatj people in the northeast corner of Australia. It refers to two parties coming together, after a struggle, to heal the wounds of the past and to work towards establishing just relations for the future. There are two crucial elements to this concept that the Council highlights. The first is the need to establish an agreement-making process between First Nations and federal and state governments – a treaty process. The second is the need for truth-telling. A Makarrata Commission would provide a mechanism and public space for 'truth telling about our history'. It's important to note how closely the call for truth-telling is linked to the proposed treaty process: it's not only about reckoning with the past, but also informing and shaping the future.[2] The renowned Australian anthropologist W. H. Stanner once said that the persistent absence of Aboriginal peoples from Australia's history constituted a 'cult of forgetfulness'.[3] The Uluru Statement demands that we abandon that cult once and for all.

What kind of statement is the 'Uluru Statement from the Heart'? Philosophers talk of statements being 'performative' when they do something in being said, as opposed to merely saying it. Political theorists, in turn, often focus on performative statements that create or found political things: for example, the force of the utterance 'We the people ...' in the preamble to the American constitution, or 'We hold these truths to be self-evident ...' in the Declaration of Independence.

All founding statements contain structural gaps between their intended meaning and the effects they seek to bring about in the world. There is no better example of this than the deep incongruity between the substance of the claims in the American Declaration of Independence and their co-existence with settler colonialism and slavery. These gaps must be filled by politics – a continual work on the world, by citizens, that returns to the promise (as yet unfulfilled) of that founding.

I believe that the Uluru Statement prefigures a possible re-founding of Australia in this sense. However, nothing is guaranteed. The initial response from the government of the day was to reject it outright. The referendum required to implement the Voice would need to be passed by a majority of the Australian people, as well as a majority of people in a majority of states. But the reaction amongst the general public has been generous, and a joint select parliamentary committee, made up of members from all sides of politics, has called for the Voice to become a reality (though there remains disagreement about how exactly that could be achieved). The Statement has thus set in motion a series of possibilities that could yet bring into being new forms of political relations between First Nations and the Australian state.

Another opportunity that has emerged is to rethink some of the normative foundations of liberal democracy in light of the Uluru Statement. Its core conceptual elements – of voice, history, truth-telling, agreement-making, legitimacy and justice – prefigure a potential normative foundation for First Nation and liberal state relations. My goal in this book is to try to develop this idea more fully, and to use the opportunity to respond to the challenge I believe Indigenous peoples present to liberal political theory more generally.

I need to make one thing clear before we begin. I am not an Aboriginal person. I grew up in Québec, Canada; was educated there and in the

United Kingdom; and have now lived and worked in Australia for almost two decades. Although I draw extensively from Aboriginal political and legal philosophy, I am writing very much from a non-Aboriginal perspective, and as someone deeply interested in the history and future of liberal political thought. But I am also writing as a citizen; as someone trying to understand these issues more fully – to try to respond to what I see as a profound challenge to the future of liberal democracy. The Uluru Statement is an outstretched hand from the Indigenous peoples of Australia to all of us – tentatively and perhaps wearily so. This short book is a modest attempt to grab hold and begin the conversation.

1

The Challenge

Introduction

Can liberal democracy accommodate the claims of Indigenous peoples? More precisely: can it do so *justly*? For it's clear that the history of relations between Indigenous peoples and liberal democratic states – especially settler colonial ones – has been a tale of woe and yet also of survival and resurgence; a history of dispossession, war, genocide, racial supremacy and political domination, but also of resistance and resilience. What are the consequences of this history? How should it be reflected in our normative thinking about political relations between Indigenous peoples and the state? Can liberalism deal with this history – *its* own history? There is a strong tendency in much contemporary political theory to develop theories that abstract

1

away from the particular histories of the various groups and actors involved in political conflict. Now, there is nothing problematic with abstraction itself. We need abstraction to construct theories in the first place. But can the demands for justice for Indigenous peoples be answered through liberal political institutions despite their deep entanglement in the history of colonialism and empire?

Indigenous peoples currently reside within the established boundaries of Australia, Canada, the United States, New Zealand, as well as countries throughout the Americas, Africa, Asia and Scandinavia. But how did they come to be in this position in the first place? How did the state's right to rule over them and their territories come to be established? On what basis has their incorporation been justified? On what basis are those boundaries legitimate? The histories of state formation are messy and bloody, far removed from the abstractions of normative political theory. As Thomas Hobbes quipped, '[T]here is scarce a Common-Wealth in the world, whose beginning can in conscience be justified.'[1]

What makes the case of Indigenous peoples so challenging for liberal states – and ultimately for liberal theories of justice – is that their claims strike at the heart of the moral foundations for claims of sovereign rule over the peoples and territories within such states' borders (as well as the foundations of international law that purports to legitimate those boundaries).

Outlining the Challenge

There are two things we must do in taking the claims of Indigenous peoples seriously. First, we need to challenge the standard assumption that the state and its boundaries are justified and hence the justificatory burden is on Indigenous peoples as to why they have the rights and powers they claim to possess. This assumption lies at the foundation of much of contemporary political theory. Instead we must ask: on what grounds is the liberal state's sovereignty and control over territory justified to Indigenous peoples? If we fail to grapple with this primary question, then many of the critical issues to do with property, or the scope of minority rights, become problematically pre-determined.

The second thing we must do is deal with the nature of *settler* colonialism. As Patrick Wolfe put it: 'Settler colonies [are] premised on the elimination of native societies.'[2] The seizure and control of territory is at the heart of settler colonialism.

The colonial justification of dispossession drew on ideologies of civilizational and racial superiority and the denigration of Indigenous political institutions, philosophies, cultural practices and ways of life. Recent scholarship has demonstrated that many of the arguments justifying the expropriation of Indigenous territories and their incorporation into the settler state also came from canonical figures in liberal political thought.[3] The history of many of the core concepts in liberalism – such as human rights, property, sovereignty and self-determination – are inextricably entangled with justifications of colonialism and empire. John Locke, Hugo Grotius, Alexis de Tocqueville, J. S. Mill, Herbert Spencer and other significant figures in the pre-history of liberalism were all engaged, to varying extents, with the colonial and imperial practices of their day. Locke, for example, in Chapter 5 of his *Two Treatises of Government* (1689), provided a justification for the settlement of the Americas on the basis that the Indigenous nations did not cultivate their lands or possess the requisite political agency from whom consent was required for the exercise of political power over them.[4]

This history of liberalism's entanglement with empire is, however, complex. Locke's *Two Treatises* is about more than just property. There are Lockean arguments that can be turned around to criticize the very claims he makes about the subjugation of Indigenous peoples – including his deep concern about arbitrary power and the tight connection he draws between political legitimacy and consent. There are also deep currents of anti-imperialism within Western political thought more generally. Philosophers and jurists worried about the consequences of imperialism abroad returning as tyranny at home. The very concept of 'occupation' that lay at the heart of claims for dispossessing Indigenous lands was flipped and used to justify counter-claims that non-European peoples had, in fact, established property and political rights through their prior occupation of physical and political space.[5]

More importantly, there was always resistance to settler colonialism. This is evident from the extensive frontier violence and wars that occurred in Canada, the United States and Australia, for example, throughout the early years of settlement. It is also clear from the hundreds of treaties that were signed between First Nations, European and American powers between 1600 and 1800.[6] Indigenous peoples fought back and argued back. They made representations before European tribunals, as well as in letters, petitions, oral presentations and statements that were often recorded by colonial authorities, as well as captured in Indigenous texts of various kinds. They negotiated directly with European powers, and in so doing, despite the treaties being broken many times over, helped shape the emerging global law of nations, as well as the constitutional orders of Anglo-American settler states.[7]

The other critical feature of settler colonialism is that the dispossession of Indigenous peoples' lands is not only something that happened in the past but is *ongoing*. It was only in 1992 that the Australian High Court recognized Aboriginal 'native title' on the continent, and only in 2019 that it recognized that compensation might be due for cultural loss as a result of dispossession.[8] Relatedly, the international legal system that has arisen from the sixteenth century onwards not only didn't halt European imperialism and colonization, but has, arguably, continued to facilitate it.[9] The current critique of the global economic and political order as a neo-liberal *Pax Americana* and as perpetuating deeply unequal economic and social relations between North and South is an extension of this concern.

Political domination and dispossession of territory are the two key elements of the deep structure of settler colonialism that liberal political theory must deal with. They represent the deep wrongs that any account of the moral foundations of the liberal state must respond to. It is important to keep both of these elements in focus at the same time.[10] Colonial settlers denied Indigenous peoples' territorial rights and sought to incorporate them into the newly established states by force – either directly, through war and other violent means, or indirectly, by allowing settlers to gradually displace and outnumber them. It's not just that settlers denied them fair terms of political association. They also violated their territory-based rights and practices.

The history of empire makes vivid what can often be a rather arid debate in political theory about the nature of global justice. European settlers often drew on the idea that the world was given to all in common to justify a right to mobility and an equal share of the 'new world' that trumped the rights of First Nations to exclude them. It's not that Indigenous peoples either had no moral obligation to accommodate newcomers in various ways (which they did), or that their political theories lacked the requisite concepts for doing so (they do). As we shall see, to claim a right to self-determination, or to exercise jurisdiction over territory, is not to say we have no moral obligations towards those outside of that territory. There are complex issues about the scope of our obligations to 'outsiders', as well as difficult moral trade-offs between our local attachments and more general ones. But what contemporary debates about global justice often miss are the historical and political circumstances in which many of the claims with which they are most concerned had their origins.

Can liberalism respond to these challenges? It is a daunting task. There is often a temptation to opt for one of two modes of reductionism here. According to the first, the entanglement with empire and colonialism runs so deep that liberalism is irrecoverable as a framework for just relations between liberal states and Indigenous peoples. According to the second, although liberalism is indeed entangled with colonialism, history and philosophy are two different things. Telling the history of our concepts is different from trying to justify them. I want to avoid both of these moves. History matters, deeply, and shapes not only the normative 'uptake' of concepts but also the way in which they are constructed and justified. It may be that, in the end, true decolonization requires breaking free from liberal political thought in radical ways. The rising influence of work influenced by Frantz Fanon and theorists from the global South, for example, might just bear that out.

And yet, at the same time, there is, I believe, still important work for liberal political theory to do – for concepts like equality, freedom, distributive justice, human rights and self-determination. These concepts still have a significant role to play in the public discourse of global and domestic politics. But they need to be reinterpreted in light of new scholarship and the rising force of Indigenous activism.

What is Liberalism?

Up until now we've been considering the capacity of liberalism to accommodate Indigenous peoples justly, but what do I mean by liberalism? What I *don't* mean by it is *neo-liberalism*: the extension of the logic of free markets to all domains of social and political life. There are undoubtedly overlaps between neo-liberalism and the broad liberal tradition, but it does not define liberalism *per se*. There are as many resources within liberalism for criticizing neo-liberalism as there are for supporting it.

Liberalism is a commodious tradition with a complex intellectual genealogy not easily characterized by philosophical and doctrinal uniformity. Duncan Bell has gone so far as to say that liberalism has no essence: the proliferation of historical figures and programmatic statements claiming to represent what liberalism *really* is should alert us to the historical contingency of its constitutive elements at any one point in time.[11] I will leave aside the epistemological claim that underlies Bell's historicist approach. His focus is very much that of an historian of political thought. But I agree with one key element of his argument: interpretations of tradition shape contemporary understandings of our political condition. But equally, our political condition also shapes the construction of tradition. The history of liberalism is thus 'a history of constant reinvention'.[12]

There are two broad clusters of liberal ideas in twentieth-century political thought that I will refer to throughout this book. The first is *libertarian liberalism*, in which a conception of 'freedom as non-interference' is the dominant focus. Libertarians see the primary task of government as securing the conditions of individual freedom, understood in the sense of a zone of non-interference around the individual, protecting them, in particular, from interference by the state. The second cluster – and the one I will be especially focused on – is *egalitarian liberalism*. Epitomized in the work of the American philosopher John Rawls (though by no means only him), this cluster of arguments seeks to reconcile freedom with social equality in both the political and economic sphere, along with a distinctive approach to the justification of the coercive power of the state.

Within this broad church of egalitarian liberalism there is a productive tension between what Jacob Levy has called the rationalist and pluralist approaches to individuals and groups.[13] The difference is, roughly, between those inclined to want to use state power to protect individuals from local group power, and those who see groups as the product of local choices and thus as protectors of freedom *against* state power. By 'rationalist', Levy means the demand that groups justify the norms and customs they draw on to exercise power over the members of their communities. And by pluralism he means associational, cultural, religious and jurisdictional pluralism, and the freedom of groups, more or less, to follow their own norms accordingly. As Levy says, liberalism is not only a philosophical account of liberty, but also a 'pair of rival but entwined social theories about where threats to freedom come from and how they can be met'.[14] As we shall see, egalitarian liberals are also responding to what John Rawls calls the 'fact of reasonable pluralism': the unavoidability of deep moral and political disagreement.[15]

Now in both cases we are dealing with a *liberal* approach to difference and state power, and so the limits of pluralism and rationalism will be given by liberal values of equality and freedom. There are stronger and weaker versions of the pluralist approach. One of the concerns liberals have is that members of groups should not be wholly subsumed by local norms and traditions but be free to criticize and even reject them as they see fit. At the furthest end of the rationalist spectrum, individual autonomy is seen as *the* foundational conception of freedom and the self. But, as we know, sometimes people describe their submission to the norms of a group or association as freely chosen, including norms that might seem, at least from the outside, deeply problematic. As a result, some liberals have questioned whether or not individuals, in these circumstances, really have chosen to live according to these beliefs. Susan Moller Okin, for example, worries about the place of women and young girls in such a pluralist account.[16] Will Kymlicka, as we'll see below, insists that any group rights granted by the state are conditional on those groups not constraining the autonomy of their members to dissent from illiberal norms. On the other hand, towards the other end of the pluralist spectrum, one finds liberals placing greater emphasis on the value of toleration, and thus protecting cultural and national minority groups from just about all forms of state interference.

I agree with Levy, however, that of primary concern in both cases should be the exercise of power as much as the focus on autonomy or toleration. And this is particularly important when thinking about Indigenous peoples in liberal democratic states. From their perspective, for both the pluralist and rationalist approaches, there is a prior question about the legitimacy of the state (and the international legal order that encompasses it) as the apparent protector of equality, freedom and toleration. Moreover, Indigenous 'groups' are better described as *polities*: they are generative sources of normative order. The history of their generative powers being denied and displaced by European and settler colonial powers means that the distinction between rationalist and pluralist approaches to liberal justice and legitimacy is less obvious than often supposed. Domination can occur directly from the state, but also indirectly

– from both the state and its agencies, but also from corporations and other sources of private power – even while apparently enjoying self-determination. The pluralism that Indigenous peoples' claims entail runs deeper than many liberal pluralists admit, and the tension between different sources of normative order is greater than many liberal rationalists can bear.

We will explore different approaches to liberal political order in the chapters to follow. For now, I want to highlight how a focus on taking the history of colonial injustice seriously is a crucial starting point for liberal egalitarian approaches to Indigenous peoples. It's not something the Rawlsian tradition, at least, has tended to do. Liberalism, in a Rawlsian mood, is inherently forward looking and not backward looking. Demands for reparations for historical injustices such as slavery or colonialism, for example, have tended to be seen as either too far in the past and so not morally justiciable – the injustices have been 'superseded' – or grounded in dubious assertions of natural rights.[17] Understanding how inequalities arose in the first place is taken to be less important than addressing injustice in the here and now.

The most important shift liberalism needs to make in order to treat Indigenous peoples justly is to embrace a more historically informed approach to justice (and injustice), both domestic and global. To see justice as either inherently backward looking or forward looking is too limiting. We need to take a diachronic approach, in which past, present and future help shape our thinking about the nature of justice. Principles of redress will need to sit alongside those of equal opportunity and the 'fair value' of the liberties. This is because the injustices faced by Indigenous peoples are enduring and structural in nature.[18]

Liberalism and Structural Injustice

What do I mean by *structural* injustice? The structural features of society that a theory of justice must reckon with are all those that shape our most important interests – including our income, health, sense of self-worth and basic freedom. It's the way the colour of your skin, your cultural background or your gender (or all three) shape your life prospects. Injustices are structural when, at least in part, institutions, norms, practices and material conditions combine to play either a causal or conditioning role in producing them. As Iris Marion Young puts it, these social structures provide the 'channels' that enable and constrain individual and collective action. Thus, a concern with structural injustice requires focusing not only on unjust *acts*, or interactions between agents, but also on the social structures within which those acts occur.[19] To do justice to an individual or group, then, must include addressing the background conditions against which people act (and interact) and the institutions and norms in which they are enmeshed. We have a general duty, according to Young, to address structural injustice, given that we are helping to sustain the conditions that produce it through our participation in the main institutions and practices of our society. This touches on deep and complex matters to do with individual and collective responsibility. It's not that we should abandon conceptions of autonomy and responsibility entirely and blame everything on structures beyond our control. We act within a complex ecology of constraints and freedoms, and thus a wholly structural or narrowly agent-centred approach is insufficient to the theoretical and practical task at hand.

Return for a moment to Rawls's conception of justice as fairness. Justice, he argues, is 'a standard whereby the distributive aspects of the basic structure of society are to be assessed'.[20] The 'basic structure', according to Rawls, is the 'background social framework within which activities of associations and individuals take place' – the way in which the main social and political institutions of society fit together into a system of social cooperation.[21] The focus here is on procedural and distributive unfairness. But people don't simply find themselves disadvantaged. Understanding the way goods are produced matters as much as how they are distributed. To become unemployed is not akin to finding one's house flooded by heavy rains, despite the fact that both are forms of disadvantage. We should indeed care about the bad luck people suffer from, but bad luck should not be the paradigmatic case of injustice.[22]

At this point, ideas of domination (and non-domination) come to the fore as possible alternatives to contemporary theories of (in)justice. Consider, once again, Young's approach. She argues that the 'distributive paradigm' needs to be supplemented by attention to both oppression and domination. Oppression consists in 'systematic institutional processes which inhibit people's ability to play and communicate with others or to express their feelings and perspectives on social life in context where others can listen'. Domination, on the other hand, 'consists in institutional conditions which inhibit or prevent people from participating or determining their actions'.[23] Justice needs to attend to both of these dimensions.

Another variation of this critique is the republican conception of 'freedom as non-domination', developed by Quentin Skinner and Philip Pettit. For Pettit, a relationship of domination exists just to the extent that A has arbitrary power over certain of B's choices.[24] By arbitrary power, Pettit means that A can obstruct, coerce or manipulate B's choices in ways that B can't meaningfully check, or which aren't 'reasoned' in the appropriate sense. This is true even if A holds those powers in reserve, so to speak, and B is able to act 'freely'. Thus B can only enjoy true non-domination in relation to A when A can't exercise power over them in both of these senses. I am not free simply because no one *actually* interferes with me: the mere *potential* for interference threatens my liberty.

What implications does this focus on structural injustice have for liberalism? There are at least two philosophical paths one could follow at this point. According to the first, you might think that we should simply bite the bullet and limit considerations of justice to essentially those of a distributive kind. Although it is tempting to extend the concept to apply to a whole range of political phenomena, the more we try to shoehorn into the scope of a theory of justice, the less real work it can do. There are other conceptual resources available to us for assessing the badness of things in the world. Domination, on this view, should best be conceived independently of injustice, just because of the way it captures something distinctive that our best theories of justice cannot. There are limits to what *liberal* theories of justice can do to address the kind of concerns identified in these critiques.

A second path, however, would entail putting domination at the centre of our concerns about justice, just because it represents the denial of a person's fundamental standing – their 'right to have rights', in Hannah Arendt's evocative phrase.[25] In other words, the first question of justice is not about distribution, but rather about the capacity of persons to demand justifications for, and partici-pation in, the processes that identify the goods to be distributed in the first place.[26] Of course, there are institutional and material preconditions for *these* capacities too, and so even here we need distributive principles. However, this approach tips our thinking about justice in a more democratic direction. If we are concerned not only with fairness and non-arbitrariness, but now also with systematic and institutionalized forms of domination, then we need to consider the particular contexts within which goods emerge, gain meaning and circulate. Our concern, therefore, should not only be with the possibility for arbitrary interference, but also with citizens (and non-citizens) being displaced from politics in ways that allow for the exercise of their effective political agency.[27]

The Intervention

Our discussion has been fairly abstract up to now. I want to conclude with an example that demonstrates the double bind of dispossession and political domination in which Indigenous peoples often find themselves, and which underlies the appeal to proposals like an Indigenous Voice to Parliament.

In June 2007, in response to a devastating report on the social conditions of Aboriginal communities in remote areas of the Northern Territory, the Australian government announced the creation of the Northern Territory Emergency Response (NTER) – referred to widely as 'the Intervention'. There had been similar reports in the past and similar howls of outrage. But the timing of its release (close to a federal election), and the deeply disturbing accounts of child and sexual abuse, alongside those of domestic violence, poverty and ill-health, intensified the political reaction. The government essentially seized control of over half the Northern Territory; it took over direct governance of seventy-three remote Aboriginal communities. The focus was meant to be on improving community healthcare as well as housing, sanitation and school facilities. But among the measures introduced were mandatory income management for Aboriginal welfare recipients; the banning of alcohol and pornography; the suspension of a permit system that controlled access to Aboriginal territories; excluding customary law from sentencing provisions; and the compulsory acquisition of some Aboriginal lands on five-year leases. The Australian army was mobilized to help implement the Intervention.

In order to pass the legislation underpinning the Intervention, the government suspended the operation of the Racial Discrimination Act (1975) – passed when Australia became a signatory to the International Convention on Social and Political Rights – and the Northern Territory's own anti-discrimination legislation. This was justified on the basis of there being a national emergency – a social welfare emergency. To many readers, no doubt, this whole episode bears the hallmarks of what the German jurist Carl Schmitt saw as lying at the heart of liberal conceptions of sovereignty: the right to declare a 'state of exception' and suspend the rule of law in order to save it.[28] For Schmitt, writing during the Weimar crisis in 1930s Germany, and who was a Nazi sympathizer, the need for sovereign dictatorship was necessary in order to overcome the inherent indeterminacy of liberal jurisprudence (something liberals failed repeatedly to grasp). Schmitt drew the wrong conclusion, but, for our purposes, the main issue raised by the Intervention is not about the ultimate coherence of liberal constitutional orders, but rather the way injustices in colonial contexts compound each other.

What does the example tell us, more generally, about the relation between justice and domination? It points to how the injustices of colonial domination are multiple and overlapping. The social and economic disadvantages suffered by Indigenous peoples, especially in remote Australia, are severe. They cry out for distributional redress. And yet they are also connected to deep and pervasive features of the Australian political system – to the history of colonialism, embedded racism, poverty and failed policies over many years. It's not that banning alcohol or pornography, for example, is itself wrong as a means of addressing a desperate social

22

situation. But the manner in which these policies are pursued and implemented is as important as the ends upon which they are justified. The injustices are structural and the responses to them need to be as well. Colonialism isn't like a flood or a snowstorm. It's not just bad luck that has landed Indigenous polities in the situation they find themselves in.

Conclusion

Are there sufficient resources within liberalism to address the challenge presented by Indigenous peoples' claims? I am not arguing that liberalism is the only framework for doing so: Indigenous, post-colonial, Marxist and post-structuralist approaches offer powerful alternatives. But nor is it time to abandon liberalism altogether. The liberal egalitarian ambition of reconciling political freedom with social equality remains a project worth pursuing, however far we seem from realizing it. Grappling with the ongoing reality of the political domination and dispossession of Indigenous peoples within existing liberal democratic states, strange as it may seem, offers a chance to reimagine contemporary liberalism.

2

Multiculturalism

Introduction

For many people, the accommodation of Indigenous peoples' political claims is often associated with the 'multicultural turn' in political theory – and in society more generally. In Australia, for example, the rejection of the racist 'White Australia' migration policy, combined with limited, but still significant, recognition of broader human rights norms in its approach to issues of racial discrimination, is often tied with the emergence of multiculturalism as a public ideal. However, Indigenous political theorists have been at pains to point out that, although connected, there are important differences between multiculturalism and First Nations' self-government and land rights. In this chapter, we explore the potential and limits of liberal multiculturalism as a framework for accommodating Indigenous peoples in liberal democracies.

Defining and Defending Multiculturalism

First of all, what do we mean by multiculturalism? It has come to refer to a broad array of theories, attitudes, beliefs, norms, practices and policies that seek to provide public recognition of and support for the accommodation of non-dominant ethnocultural groups. The nature of these non-dominant groups will vary: some may be immigrant minorities (including refugees), others will be 'historically settled' minorities, such as national minorities (e.g. the Québécois), or indeed Indigenous peoples. These differences are important, as we shall see. However, what is distinctive about multiculturalism – and especially *liberal* multiculturalism – is the desire to go beyond the protection of basic civil and political liberties associated with liberal citizenship, to forms of differentiated citizenship that allow groups to express their distinct identities and practices in various ways.[1] Some of these measures include the recognition and support of minority languages, exemptions from generally applicable laws and the recognition of 'inherent rights of

25

self-government'. This means debates about multiculturalism inevitably involve deeper claims about not only the vexed question of culture, but also the nature of freedom, equality, democracy and justice.

It is important to acknowledge an immediate problem with this broad conception of multiculturalism. What it means (and prospects for its future) can vary from place to place. This is particularly true when comparing attitudes towards multiculturalism in many parts of Western and Eastern Europe; in North, Central and South America; in Australasia; and also, increasingly, in Africa and Asia. Some of this is to do with different facts on the ground, and some to do with different histories of settlement and forms of nation building. Context is crucial; although we can pick out certain broad elements that most forms of liberal multiculturalism share, there will also always be important differences too. In Canada and Australasia, for example, 'multiculturalism' is not generally used to refer to the situation of Indigenous peoples, as there is a prior question about the legitimacy of the state, as we shall see. Elsewhere, however, such as in Latin America, 'multiculturalism' includes the claims of Indigenous peoples, as well as other ethnocultural groups.

There are, I believe, three broad approaches to multiculturalism in contemporary political theory.

The first is *protective* or *communitarian* multiculturalism. The basic idea here is that the central point of any form of public recognition or accommodation of a group is to preserve the cultural integrity and authenticity of its way of life. This is often accompanied by a reified sense of culture, which is reduced to a discrete set of traditional practices assumed to be at the heart of the group's identity. Thus, in order to protect the individuals, you must preserve the group, and that means protecting their culture. The right to preserve one's cultural authenticity is assumed then to preclude others from making judgements about those practices, including appealing to universal standards of justice or human rights. The legitimacy of the exercise of authority within these groups, along with the legitimacy of various internal practices, is a matter for the group to adjudicate and nobody else.

The second approach is *liberal* multiculturalism, which has been far and away the most prominent in recent political theory. There are many variations of liberal multiculturalism, but the basic idea is something like this: multiculturalism is justified as an approach to cultural and religious diversity because doing so promotes liberal values such as equality, autonomy, toleration and equal respect. Thus, although liberal multiculturalism may well enable degrees of cultural preservation or protectionism, that isn't its central aim. The extent of cultural preservation will be a function of the degree to which it helps promote liberal ends. Liberal multiculturalism is also universalist in orientation: the value of autonomy or equality that underpins it is valuable for everyone, whatever their cultural background. Thus, those practices that undermine a person's autonomy, or basic human rights, are not entitled to protection or accommodation. Moreover, liberal multiculturalism aims explicitly at transforming current social and political arrangements, and especially the cultural dimensions of these arrangements. It seeks to transform the way dominant majorities have treated minorities within their boundaries, as well as the way minority groups ought to press their claims. It seeks to transform the identities and practices of both minority and majority groups, in line with liberal democratic norms of anti-discrimination, equality and basic human rights. It aims to do so by ensuring that minorities enjoy the 'fair value' of their basic civil and political liberties, to use John Rawls's phrase, by providing differentiated rights tailored to the specific circumstances of the groups in question. Now, liberal multiculturalists accept that simply imposing liberal democratic practices on groups is, in many circumstances, unjustified and impractical. But, ultimately, illiberal practices (whether those of minorities or majorities) ought to be transformed. Liberal multiculturalism is superior to monoculturalism (liberal or otherwise) because it increases the range of choices and options available to individuals. This means diversity isn't valuable in itself for the liberal, but rather it has value because it is correlative with liberty, and thus crucial for the development of individual autonomy.

The third approach to multiculturalism is neither protective nor liberal, and not really a normative stance at all, but rather a *critical perspective* on it. According to this view, multiculturalism is essentially a new version of the hierarchical and racialized modes of political order that it was supposed to have displaced. It presents a critical lens through which to analyse the various relations of power that operate via forms of liberal 'government'. Critics of multiculturalism are often concerned with the limits of multicultural accommodation, and especially the practical consequences of 'really existing liberal multiculturalism'. In particular, they point to the ways in which liberal accommodation is essentially *conditional*: cultures that qualify for rights are assumed to be homogeneous and bounded (even as the liberal state is pluralized), and minorities are expected not to challenge the basic legitimacy of the state, as well as to live up to pre-conceived notions of what a ' good migrant' or 'indigenous person' is supposed to be. Liberal legal pluralism, on this reading, is basically a means of re-subordinating marginal groups within a legal system that leaves their substantive disadvantage intact. It might be a subtle and less heavy-handed form of pluralism than earlier forms of colonialism, but liberal multi-cultural 'government' (understood in the broadest sense of the term) is basically continuous with it.[2] Even more broadly, insofar as this analysis of multi-culturalism puts power at the heart of its analysis, it raises questions about the way in which 'minorities' and 'majorities' are defined and produced in the first place. Who is the 'we' who tolerates 'them', and what are the underlying assumptions about who or what can be accommodated and why?

Each of these approaches picks out a distinctive strand of both the academic and public discourse surrounding multiculturalism. There can be 'harder' and 'softer' versions of all three. For example, one can find forms of *protective liberal* multicultur-alism amongst theorists and policy makers for whom cultural difference is the crucial variable in addressing disadvantage. Within this quadrant there are a range of variations: some modes of protective liberalism license greater intervention in cultural practices to promote liberal ends, others almost none, save for the right to exit. Some liberals base their arguments on the value of autonomy, others on toleration. An analysis of *imperial liberal* multiculturalism, on the other hand, might focus on the conditions surrounding multicultural citizenship. Or it might question the very ontology of liberal conceptions of 'minorities' and 'majorities' altogether.

And so what is the proper *subject* of multiculturalism: individuals, groups, cultures, or peoples? Or some combination thereof? Any approach to multiculturalism must deal with the nature of groups and the issues they raise for liberal democratic politics.

Liberal Multiculturalism and Its Critics

The canonical liberal response to diversity (especially religious diversity) has three basic features: the neutrality of the state; equal treatment in terms of non-discrimination; and the privatization of religious belief as a matter of individual conscience. Although religious diversity remains important, the scope of diversity has been radically extended – including now cultural and ethnic groups, racial groups, national groups, linguistic minorities, as well as differences based on gender, sexuality and disability. The claim that liberal democratic states like the United States or Canada can somehow remain ethnoculturally neutral is also under pressure: the history of the way territorial boundaries have been drawn, the way national symbols are chosen and used in the public culture, the dominance of a national language, among other things, all seem to point beyond state neutrality.[3]

One way to understand these developments is as part of the gradual extension of citizenship rights. If the struggle for equal citizenship throughout the nineteenth and twentieth centuries involved extending the rights of citizenship to encompass a greater number of people (workers, women and migrants), as well as across a broader range of entitlements (civil, political, social and economic), then the demand for multicultural citizenship is simply another step along this path. Multiculturalism is thus not a break with liberal citizenship, but rather the logical extension of it in conditions of deep diversity.

The basic claim at the heart of liberal multiculturalism is that certain social and cultural identities deserve to be recognized because, without them, individuals lack something they need for living decent lives. If human beings are always culturally embedded beings, then equal respect for individuals means equal respect for the cultural structures and forms of life they create, sustain and value. There are two important moves here. The first has to do with the appeal to equality. The second has to do with the relation between individuals and groups. Let's explore this a bit further.

The first move is the suggestion that the accommodation of cultural, national, religious or ethnic difference is connected to a rich sense of equality. Recall that according to liberal neutrality, we treat someone equally when we respect and protect their basic rights. Lying behind this idea is an appeal to the connection between equality and treating people similarly. Of course, equality is always a matter of treating like cases alike, and that means deciding what are the relevant cases to consider. But on the richer view, we treat someone equally when they have the resources to enjoy the fair value of their basic rights, as well as genuine equality of opportunity. In a culturally diverse society, members of both majority and minority groups may well have very different capacities and needs that are relevant to judging whether someone enjoys genuine equality of opportunity. A disabled person, for example, may need to be treated differently than an able-bodied person in order to be treated with genuine equal respect. Both are entitled to equal civic liberties, but a disabled person may require more resources in order to realize the equal value of their freedom. The interesting cases are when this analogy is extended to cultural and national groups. Are there forms of accommodation or protection for minority groups that can be justified on the grounds of promoting equality?

There is a related question about different kinds of disadvantage an individual or group might suffer from, and therefore what forms of compensation or public policy might be justified in addressing them. As we saw in Chapter 1, critics of liberalism argue that a problem with adopting state neutrality is that it fails to address forms of inequality that are the product of certain structural features of society. The same argument is applied to multi-culturalism. Iris Marion Young, for example, has distinguished between two forms of 'the politics of difference'.[4] The first involves 'positional difference' and the second 'cultural difference'. Positional difference refers to the way individuals are structured by various kinds of norms, practices and institutions. That is, it refers to the way norms and practices are reproduced in society through, say, the division of labour, or various decision-making processes that systematically disadvantage certain groups by inhibiting the development of their capacities. These structural inequalities persist despite people enjoying the same (formal) civil and political liberties. Recall the example above to do with disabled people. Young's claim is that this isn't simply a case of them lacking the capacities required to lead fulfilling lives, but rather a problem with the practices and norms of the rest of society that prevents them from exercising their capacities to their fullest extent. What constitutes the 'normal range' of valuable human functioning, for example, includes facts about the built environment, social expectations and attitudes, aesthetic standards, and so on, that have real consequences for disabled people to be able to lead decent lives. Similar claims can be made about the persistence of institutional racism and the gendered division of labour. Thus, even with the extension of basic civil and political liberties to members of previously excluded social and cultural groups, the structural features of society prevent genuine equality being realized for these citizens.

The important point here is that to address positional difference requires going well beyond 'difference-blind' or neutralist liberalism. But it's also a *structural* difference as opposed to a cultural one, and so focusing on cultural difference might well also leave structural disadvantage inadequately addressed. Cultural differences present another set of challenges. Here inequality can exist in virtue of the relation between the dominant 'societal culture' and minority cultural groups. The ability of minority cultural groups to sustain their cultural practices can become more difficult, and if this is mainly as a result of the circumstances members face, as opposed to the choices they've made, then the situation is potentially unfair. The dominant group can limit the opportunities of other groups to realize their ends, whether through explicit repression, or merely by growing or allowing minority practices to wither away. Of course, cultural change is not in itself something that can (or should) be prevented; the case for sustaining minority cultural practices will depend on the connection between their survival and the well-being of the minority group's members.

Note that these two approaches to disadvantage are clearly not mutually exclusive, despite what some of the literature suggests. Members of a minority cultural group might well suffer from various structural forms of inequality too. Feminist analyses of the situation of women and girls within minority groups, for example, bring this out very clearly.[5] However, depending on the nature of the disadvantage with which you are concerned, different solutions and approaches may be called for, and tensions between different approaches can emerge. A move to provide more autonomy for national minorities, for example, will require finding ways of ensuring vulnerable members *within* those groups are treated equally and can exercise their freedom in meaningful ways. Focusing on disadvantage through the lens of structural disadvantage tends to shift discussion towards ideals of democratic citizenship that cut across cultural and national differences. Focusing on the accommodation of cultural differences, on the other hand, tends to shift discussion towards forms of collective autonomy and freedom. Any adequate analysis of the challenge of diversity will require a subtle interweaving of the two.

Up until now, we have been moving between ideas of what is owed to individuals and groups, as if this relation was relatively unproblematic. Remember that one of the crucial moves we identified above was equal respect for *persons* being extended to equal respect for *cultures* or *groups*. But we need an argument to link these two claims; one does not follow automatically from the other. The tension is neatly demonstrated in the frequent slippage between talking about the 'rights of minority cultures' and the 'rights of cultural minorities'. Are cultures the kind of things that can have rights? Or are we instead concerned only with the rights of the individual members of those groups?

Justifying Liberal Multiculturalism

One of the most influential arguments linking the well-being of individuals with the public recognition of minority groups has been provided by the Canadian political theorist Will Kymlicka. For Kymlicka, access to a secure cultural structure provides individuals with a 'context for choice'. Culture, in other words, or at least what he calls a 'societal culture', helps people realize their autonomy – their freedom. This is a universalist claim about the value of autonomy for everyone. A societal culture is basically a territorially concentrated culture, centred on a shared language used in a wide range of societal institutions in both public and private life (schools, media, law, economy, government, etc.).[6] Thus, a societal culture is different from a set of religious beliefs or personal lifestyles: skateboarders may well share a common subculture, but they don't share a societal culture. Societal cultures are, however, inevitably pluralistic; they will often include people with different religious faiths, sexual orientations and class differences. However, this pluralism is balanced by a degree of linguistic, institutional and territorial cohesion.

Many social scientists have criticized Kymlicka for this seemingly homogeneous and bounded conception of culture, however much he has used it to try to pluralize the nation-state. But for our purposes, it's important to see how he thinks access to a societal culture and freedom are connected. Providing groups with support for the preservation of their societal culture is something that not only extends a privilege larger groups already enjoy (often unknowingly), but also helps promote important liberal goods. What is being protected through self-government rights or language rights, therefore, is not the particular *content* of any culture, but rather the *structure* within which people exercise their freedom and through which they make sense of the world.

Kymlicka's argument is not the only one to link cultural membership with liberal values. And indeed, many have criticized it for appealing to a value – autonomy – that might not be as universal as he thinks. Charles Taylor, for example, sees 'recognition' as a crucial human good, given the way it is linked to forms of personal and collective identity that enable common deliberation about the nature of the good in the first place.[7] Because our sense of self is shaped by the recognition (and indeed *mis*recognition) of others, the way the group I identify with is recognized politically and institutionally matters too. For Taylor, our identities are fundamentally intersubjective, and this has important consequences for thinking about how we ought to manage the deep diversity of modern societies. (We will explore his argument in Chapter 4.)

The most important forms of group membership are those that provide people with access to valuable human goods. For many people, these forms of identity are not easily shed, but nor are they so constraining as to be necessarily incompatible with liberal freedom. For Kymlicka, as well as other defenders of liberal multiculturalism, the main task, then, is to distinguish between ways of accommodating diversity that are compatible with liberal ends, and those that are not.

Thus, according to Kymlicka, groups that violate their members' basic liberties, or prevent them from exercising their autonomy, are not entitled to multicultural accommodation (although how we handle these situations in reality is a separate issue). At this point, for many critics, liberal multiculturalism begins to look less multicultural and more about defending a particular liberal way of life. As we've seen, for some liberals, this is hardly a contradiction: the whole point of liberal multiculturalism is to transform the way states engage with minority groups and how they, in turn, treat their members. But the critique of liberal neutrality also points to a deeper critique of liberalism itself. And here we reach a critical point in the analysis of the relation between the claims of Indigenous peoples and multiculturalism.

Multiculturalism and Indigenous Peoples

There are two fundamental challenges that Indigenous peoples' claims present for liberal multiculturalism.

The first is that insofar as a claim for liberal justice is tied to the existence of a distinctive minority culture and the role it plays in supporting individual autonomy, much will ride on the characterization of the cultural group. In the case of First Nations, recognition will depend, in part, on empirical questions about the viability of their cultural structures, the fragility of which is a result of the very injustice multiculturalism is meant to address. Courts in Australia and Canada, for example, have often tied the legal validity of 'Aboriginal title' – Aboriginal property rights – to a continuing connection to the land by the group and their ability to maintain their cultural practices over time.[8] And yet, as we have seen, given the consequences of hundreds of years of dispossession, this means that only a limited number of claims have any chance of being vindicated. If the viability of a cultural structure is a condition for being recognized by the state, the legacy of colonialism often renders that right meaningless.

The deeper problem is the underlying assumed legitimacy of the multicultural state. If liberal multiculturalism is premised on *the state* granting recognition to a minority group's claims for self-government or autonomy, then there is the prior question of the ultimate source of Indigenous peoples' right to self-government. Indigenous sovereignty is an assertion of autonomy that is not dependent on the grant of that authority from any other entity. This is what Indigenous and various Canadian legal theorists refer to as the 'inherent right of self-government'.[9] Despite the lack of respect for this Indigenous sovereignty by settler liberal states, Indigenous nations have continued to understand the source of these claims to derive from their own laws and normative orders, and not from those of the states to which they have been subject.

For example, James Anaya argues that the term 'indigenous' refers to 'the living descendants of pre-invasion inhabitants of lands now dominated by others. ... They are indigenous because their ancestral roots are embedded in the lands in which they live ... much more deeply than the roots of more powerful sectors of society living on the same lands or in close proximity.'[10] However, it is also important not to restrict our understanding of the jurisdiction and rights of Indigenous peoples to being mainly about property, as important as that is. Just as important is the continuity of the legal and normative orders within which concepts of land and community live, despite the disruption brought about by colonialism. The assertion of the reality of these legal and normative orders by Indigenous peoples has been a critical part of their ongoing resistance.

To his credit, Kymlicka has recognized the force of this critique and emphasized the extent to which the denial of Indigenous self-government points to the injustice inherent in the nation-building practices of liberal democratic states like Canada and Australia. If the dominant majority had a right to engage in nation-building, why should this be denied to other peoples who are only a 'minority' as a result of being unfairly incorporated into the state?

So, as important as the multicultural turn has been for contemporary political theory and practice, there are severe limits to applying it to the case of Indigenous peoples. In particular, we need to make sense of how Aboriginal sovereignty persists alongside that of the liberal state. The persistence of normative pluralism is often taken to be a sign not only of the absence of a settled constitutional and political order but even of illiberalism. However, in genuinely multicultural and multinational societies, we should see this normative pluralism as the starting point – rather than the terminus – of new forms of democratic community.

One interesting way of grasping the challenge of this normative pluralism is through the concept of rights. The discourse of rights has been powerfully co-opted and used by Indigenous peoples in domestic and international political forums for hundreds of years. If liberal multiculturalism seems to presume too much of what stands in need of justification, is there a liberal conception of rights that can be redeemed in a way that does justice to their claims? This will be the focus of our next chapter.

3

Rights

Introduction

In the previous chapter, we explored one way liberal democracy can accommodate Indigenous peoples: through liberal multiculturalism. However attractive and important an ideal this might be as a general approach to pluralism, we found it insufficient, without significant revision, when applied to their case.

Another liberal approach is to focus more closely on the nature of the claims Indigenous people seem to be making: *rights* claims. Rights lie deep in the foundations of liberalism. Indeed, for many, liberalism just is a political theory about the rights individuals have and the kind of political society required to protect them.

But the languages and practice of Indigenous

peoples' rights (or 'Aboriginal rights' – I shall use these terms interchangeably) are extensive and go back to the very first encounters between them and European colonialists. As we saw in Chapter 1, among the arsenal of arguments that Indigenous peoples mounted against settlers' claims for territory and jurisdiction were counter-claims asserting their pre-existing property and jurisdictional rights. They were, of course, adapting this language to the circumstances, as Western conceptions of 'rights' don't fully capture the complex nature of their relationships to land, the natural world and each other.[1] But the language of 'Aboriginal rights' came to be recognized – imperfectly and often fleetingly – through the emerging common and constitutional law of states such as Canada and the United States (and later in Australia) around which grew a distinctive form of intercultural domestic and international law. The Anishinabek legal philosopher John Borrows, for example, refers to Canada as having three distinct but intertwined sources of legal order: civil law, common law and Indigenous law.[2] Each has its own distinctive method for development and application, and each is relevant to the extent it develops under changing circumstances. The key is the extent to which a tradition remains a living, contemporary, complex system, as opposed to becoming inflexible and static in orientation and application. For Borrows, although Indigenous legal orders have ancient roots, 'they can also speak to the present and future needs of all Canadians'.[3] They aren't perfect and shouldn't be romanticized. But they have the capacity to be reimagined to deal with contemporary circumstances and conflict.

Is there normative and political space for Indigenous rights in liberal democracy's legal and political institutions? And what kind of rights are they? Are they legal rights granted by the state? Are they human rights adapted and shaped according to the circumstances and self-understanding of Indigenous peoples? Or are they specific cultural rights, exclusive to members of Indigenous societies? From the perspective of Indigenous peoples, their rights stem from their collective self-understandings and their legal, political and philosophical traditions and practices. And they are justified with reference to those traditions. As grasped by non-Indigenous legal systems, they refer to a complex amalgam of common law rights, treaty rights (where relevant) and human rights. I shall try to lay out these various lineaments below. But what makes them *Aboriginal* rights as opposed to simply rights? How do they fit with other kinds of human rights, liberal citizenship rights, or right to self-determination?

In the Preface, I suggested that one conceptual innovation liberalism requires is a reconciliation of historical and normative approaches to justice. Reflecting on the nature of Aboriginal rights brings this to the fore. Are Aboriginal rights the ancient, historical rights of Indigenous peoples, tied to the forms of life and practices that pre-date their encounter with European settlers? Or are they – to borrow a term from the Canadian legal theorist Brian Slattery – *generative* rights, which, although grounded in a particular history, can grow, adapt, change and renew themselves in light of new circumstances?[4] Courts have tended to see Aboriginal rights more like the former: almost frozen in time, lacking the characteristics of more abstract and normative conceptions of rights.[5] Liberal political theorists have sometimes seen them in this light too. Jeremy Waldron, for example, links claims about the relevance of 'indigeneity' to Robert Nozick's much criticized 'entitlement theory' of justice.[6] Nozick opens his book *Anarchy, State, and Utopia* – a conservative riposte to egalitarian liberalism – with the claim: 'Individuals have rights, and there are things no person or group may do to them (without violating their rights).'[7] This strong claim about individual rights entails a minimal conception of the state with strict 'side constraints' on the redistribution of wealth, including property. But it also links property rights to a theory of acquisition, transfer and rectification that places enormous emphasis on first occupation and tracing a 'clean' title to property from there. Now, although there is a superficial similarity between an entitlement theory of property and Aboriginal claims to prior occupancy, this doesn't capture in any real sense Aboriginal conceptions of property and the moral and ethical obligations that flow from them (including towards non-Aboriginal peoples). Taking history seriously does not mean embracing a deeply conservative interpretation of rights.

I shall argue that Aboriginal rights are indeed generative rights and not merely historical ones. How should liberal political theory respond to them?

The Nature of Rights

As we saw in Chapter 2, Aboriginal rights are often conceived of as cultural rights, and thus as group rights. As a result, they are vulnerable to at least three kinds of objections: first, that culture is not a 'primary good' relevant to the currency of egalitarian justice; second, that group rights are inimical to the moral individualism of liberal democratic societies; and, third, that pandering to group interests provides incentives for political abuse and undermines the conditions required for promoting liberal egalitarian outcomes. I shall try to address each of these objections below. Before doing so, however, let's begin by considering the nature of rights more broadly.

There is no definitive or categorical account of a right, and yet rights discourse is one of the most powerful in contemporary domestic and global politics. For some, rights have deep conceptual and normative roots in the kinds of people and institutions characteristic of liberal democratic societies: free, dynamic, individualistic and pluralistic. Rights stem from our inherently equal human agency. In this sense, they are foundational to, and can be used as a means of evaluating the legitimacy and moral rightness (or wrongness) of, our political institutions and practices. For others, the connection between rights and human agency is more contingent. Relations of power are constitutive of social and political practices and thus so too are our practices of rights. Hence rights may serve a strategic function in politics, but are not foundational, and thus should enjoy no privileged analytical or normative position within it. On this view, rights are derivative of a more basic account of human well-being, theory of justice or power.[8]

If one's understanding of rights is something like the first – attached to a distinctive conception of the liberal self – then the problem of whether there are any Aboriginal rights is potentially acute. What work does the modifier 'Aboriginal' do? There may be conceptual and normative constraints on what you understand a right to be, such that the very idea of an *Aboriginal* right is deeply confused. On the other hand, if your view tends towards the second, as mine does – that rights are a social and political practice, albeit an important one – then you are faced with a similar type of question, but this time from a very different direction: what is *the point* of appealing to the language of rights, given that it offers only a contingent and highly contestable source of support for the kinds of claims that Indigenous peoples are making? Rights are valuable, I shall argue, to the extent that they protect or promote certain crucial interests that individuals and groups have. These interests have to be important enough to impose duties on others to either perform or forbear from certain kinds of actions, and, at least in principle, be (at least potentially) legally enforceable. This is true of both negative and positive rights, since even negative rights of forbearance – for example, property rights – require active governmental protection and intervention.

Aboriginal and non-Aboriginal theorists, as well as those on the left and the right, are often sceptical about Aboriginal rights. The conceptual trimmers fear inflation and worry about linking the notion of rights to culturally specific claims, since this detracts from their universality. Some theorists, such as Kahnawà:ke political theorist Taiaiake Alfred, argue that Aboriginal rights are merely the 'benefits accrued by Indigenous peoples who have agreed to abandon their autonomy in order to enter the legal and political framework of the state'.[9] In Australia, Noel Pearson, a prominent Aboriginal leader and lawyer, has argued that the focus on Aboriginal rights, and especially the right to self-determination, has deflected attention from the deep social and economic problems afflicting Indigenous communities. It might have even made things worse.

These are powerful criticisms and point to how rights exist within various kinds of relations of power, as opposed to always standing over them. But before evaluating them, let's try to clarify what a right is.

A rights claim has a quadripartite structure.[10] To say A has a right to X is to commit yourself to providing an account of: (i) who or what the subject of the entitlement is; (ii) what the substance of the entitlement is; (iii) what the basis of the entitlement is; and (iv) what the purpose of the entitlement is. Thus, two of the most influential analytic accounts of rights in recent years in liberal political theory – the 'choice' and 'interest' accounts – reflect different substantive relationships between these variables. According to the choice account, for example, the concept of a right refers to an uncontested and protected domain of choice for the individual. To be a rights bearer is to have control in the sense of being able to demand or waive the performance of an action. Thus, to protect the 'integrity' of rights, and particularly the pre-emptory value of choice, rights should be seen as a set of protected options – or negative freedoms – that stand independently of other kinds of interests.

According to the interest account, on the other hand, the value of choice may be an important interest, but not necessarily the most important, and thus will have to be balanced against other values. To say A has a right to X is to say that someone else has a duty to perform some act (or omission) that is in A's interest. The interest has to be such that its protection or advancement can be accepted as a reason sufficient for holding some other person (or persons) to be under a duty. This moves us much more directly into the domain of contested moral beliefs than the choice theory does (which presupposes, for example, that our interest in having more choices rather than less is determinative) and, on my view, is all the more persuasive because of it. The interest approach also brings to the fore the mutability and contestability of 'interests', and thus of rights, and highlights the inherent indeterminacy and ultimately political nature of rights claims. As we shall see, this indeterminacy also offers room for the adaptation of our practices of rights to new circumstances and contexts.

What are Aboriginal Rights?

I believe the interest theory of rights provides a productive way of thinking about the nature of Aboriginal rights. Our challenge, then, is to understand what the crucial interests at stake are. As a first step, let's return to the notion of Aboriginal rights. I have argued that they are generative rights and not merely historical ones. But what does this mean? Consider three approaches.

First, you could argue that Aboriginal rights are essentially legal rights, granted by colonial authorities in the interests of effective colonial government, but which then evolved to acquire normative potency as beliefs about Indigenous peoples in the wider community changed.[11] Second, you could appeal to the deep historical, cultural and political specificity of the interests to which the claims refer – in other words, to Indigenous difference. And, third, you might turn to general or human rights and argue that Aboriginal rights are a species of human rights that refer to interests that everyone deserves to have protected or promoted (*qua* being human, as opposed to being Aboriginal).

The difficulty with the first approach is that it presupposes the centrality of the state. It makes rights too dependent on the assumption of the legitimacy of existing states, however much Indigenous peoples are inescapably entwined – practically, conceptually, politically – with them. Note also, though, some of the dangers in choosing the second approach, to the exclusion of any other. If Indigenous peoples are owed rights on the grounds of their radical 'otherness' from Europeans and of their having suffered grievous harm as a result of this otherness, then it is not clear whether, if their circumstances change, or their traditions evolve and adapt to new circumstances, the grounds for their rights claims are thereby undermined. A reference to Indigenous difference is vulnerable to being transformed into a claim about the exclusively historical nature of the rights in question – and suffocatingly so.

Thus, some combination of the second and third approaches seems a more promising route to travel, but each raises various difficulties along the way.

Consider, first, the 'common law doctrine of Aboriginal rights', which has been developed by a range of Canadian and Indigenous legal theorists and historians, and that we touched on in Chapter 1.[12] This doctrine refers to those rights possessed by Aboriginal peoples as they were recognized in the custom generated by relations between First Nations and incoming French and English settlers in North America from the seventeenth century onwards. According to Brian Slattery, the 'doctrine of Aboriginal rights' is a basic principle of Canadian common law which 'defines the constitutional links between the Crown and Aboriginal peoples and regulates the interplay between Canadian systems of law and government and native land rights, customary laws and political institutions'.[13] The doctrine emerged out of three broad sets of circumstances: first, the realities of life in North America in the seventeenth and eighteenth centuries and the uneasy interdependency that often existed between colonial and Aboriginal societies; second, the broad rules of equity and convenience; and, finally, changing imperial policy. The emergent principles 'were part of a special branch of British law that governed the Crown's relations with its overseas dominions, commonly termed "colonial law" or "imperial constitutional law"'.[14] These rules, Slattery claims, form a body of unwritten law known as 'the doctrine of Aboriginal rights' (the part dealing specifically with land being the 'doctrine of Aboriginal title', and the other parts dealing with treaties, customary law, powers of self-government and the fiduciary role of the Crown). The crucial legal point is that this doctrine applied automatically to a new colony when it was acquired and 'supplied the presumptive legal structure governing the position of native peoples'. In other words, 'the doctrine was part of a body of funda-mental constitutional law that was logically prior to the introduction of English common law . . . [and] limits and moulds the application of that law to native peoples'.[15] Slattery argues that this provides the legal basis for the survival of 'native customary law' in Canada (as it does, by analogy, in Australia as well). This doctrine was referred to by the courts in varying degrees from the nineteenth century onwards, but only really came into play in Canada with the *Calder* decision in 1973 and in Australia with the *Mabo* decision in 1992.[16]

On this reading, the doctrine of Aboriginal rights is thus a body of inter-societal law – a 'bridge constructed from both sides', as the landmark Canadian *Report of the Royal Commission on Aboriginal Peoples* put it. The rights to which it refers – to land, to fish and hunt, to cultural integrity, to conclude treaties, to the continuity of Aboriginal law and to the right of self-government – are 'inherent' in that they originate 'from the collective lives and traditions of these people themselves rather than from the Crown or Parliament', and are to be 'interpreted flexibly so as to permit their evolution over time'.[17] They coexist with those of the Crown and do not derive from them.[18] John Borrows refers to this body of law in the Canadian context as helping constitute Canada's 'Indigenous Constitution'.

One way of understanding Aboriginal rights, then, is to think of them as a complex bundle of common law and constitutional rights that emerged from imperfect practices of treaty-making and which are already inside the law, albeit hidden in various ways. The inherent normative ideal here is one in which the common law embodies a context-sensitive and inter-societal model for cross-cultural negotiations. But there are two ways of making sense of this ideal. For James Tully, the norms emerge out of the *actual* negotiations between peoples in the particular historical and political circumstances they find themselves in. Aboriginal rights, according to his argument, emerge out of – but at the same time come to condition – treaty negotiations between Indigenous peoples and the state. For Jacob Levy, on the other hand, a common law approach presupposes the legitimacy of the extant sovereignty of the Crown, but nevertheless, through treaties and other forms of negotiations, offers a hospitable structure within which Aboriginal interests can be accommodated.[19]

In both cases, we return to two challenges I flagged above. If it is Aboriginal difference that justifies the interests that Aboriginal rights protect, then the risk is that this may tether these rights too tightly to practices and institutions associated with Aboriginal societies prior to their contact with European ones. For example, should an Aboriginal right to fish in certain waters extend only to 'ceremonial' purposes, or include the right to fish commercially (a question tested repeatedly in Canadian and American courts in recent years)? On the other hand, if the common law (or constitution) presupposes the legitimacy of the extant sovereignty of the Crown, then when did Aboriginal peoples give up those self-government rights? How did they come to be extinguished, and on what basis? And if the presumptions of Aboriginal peoples having surrendered their sovereignty are based on now discredited beliefs, then on what basis can the state's rule over them be considered legitimate?

Hence the attraction of broadening our understanding of Aboriginal rights to include reference to more abstract principles associated with human and political rights, albeit interpreted in light of the history of settler colonialism. If Aboriginal peoples have rights as peoples to self-determination in international law, or according to the values of freedom and equality, then the common law incorporation of Aboriginal rights can be understood differently. If Indigenous peoples were sovereign and self-determining at the time of settlement, then Crown sovereignty can only be reconciled with their sovereignty through some mechanism of consent, or at least through means consistent with their freedom and equality. History tells us that this didn't occur, but the ideal can serve as a counterfactual for rethinking relations in the present.

The interests to which Aboriginal rights refer are a bundle of specific rights to do with control over their territories and the various activities that occur on them; with political rights of self-government, and with their rights as citizens of both Aboriginal nations and the wider political community in which they reside. The interests will be normatively compelling insofar as they protect and promote the basic interests of Indigenous peoples, both individually and collectively. The duty of protecting these rights falls upon Aboriginal governments, the state, Aboriginal and non-Aboriginal people, as well as the international community.

Objections

Still, there are a number of objections to this concept of Aboriginal rights that we need to consider, especially since some of the most powerful come from liberal egalitarian critics.

One objection is the extent to which 'Aboriginal rights' diverts rights too far away from their apparently tight relation to individual choice and freedom. The problem with this objection is that it presupposes there is indeed a common currency of rights that binds them almost exclusively to individual choice and freedom – which there isn't. However, another variation of this objection is potentially more powerful. Here the concern is that Aboriginal rights are inherently collective in nature, and if so, they violate the essentially individualistic nature of rights and the moral individualism of liberalism more generally. Conversely, if liberal rights are inherently individualistic, and Aboriginal political theories are not, then, from an Aboriginal perspective, they are ill-suited to promoting Aboriginal ends.

However, this isn't an objection at the level of the very concept of a right, as there is no necessary reason why we can't assign rights to groups: among the things individuals value are the groups they belong to, and thus it's plausible to think this will justify various kinds of collective rights. Moreover, as we saw in Chapter 2, there are eminently liberal grounds for thinking collective rights are not only permissible, but even required, in order to secure the freedom of members of minority groups, among others.

The more precise worry, I believe, is about the *kind* of group rights that Aboriginal rights might entail, and whether these are consistent with liberal equality more generally. Let's look at this question a bit more carefully.

As we've seen, rights are reason-dependent claims. They aren't self-justifying. We need to offer reasons as to why others should be held accountable for the duties that enable us to exercise our rights. And these reasons draw on both individual and societal interests. A right to free speech, for example, can be defended in terms of its value for the development of individual autonomy, as well as in terms of securing the benefits of democratic government. A right to property can be justified in terms of the value of individual freedom, but also in terms of promoting economic prosperity. These arguments refer not only to the interests of the right holder, but also to society more generally.

To be sure, the rights mentioned above also immunize the choices and decisions of individuals from state interference and from the smothering conformity of society. And there are indeed rights best justified with reference to the interests of individuals alone. But it is difficult to detach the value of individual rights entirely from collective and public goods. Freedoms of speech, assembly and religion all contribute to the good of democratic legitimacy and liberal toleration. On the other hand, although liberal rights can promote freedom of thought and action, their presence is not a sufficient condition for freedom to be fully realized. Rights can block intrusive social norms but also become entwined with them. Certain kinds of speech (e.g. 'hate speech') may fall outside the moral and cultural bounds of individual rights to freedom of speech. And a right to be immunized from certain kinds of state interference might embody particular assumptions about the proper role of government, or assumptions about the distinction between public and private. Thus, where a dominant culture exerts a strong or even hegemonic influence over a public culture, individual rights may do little to promote or protect diversity. Dominant languages drive out minority ones when the cost of protecting or promoting the latter becomes too high. Communal ownership of land can be made increasingly difficult in a legal and political system that strongly promotes individual ownership.

And so, the relation between group and individual rights is complex. Sometimes group interests are best protected by assigning legal rights to individuals, such as when we protect the collective right of a group by assigning legal rights to individual members to engage in group-specific activities. At other times, a group right can protect group interests by being assigned to the group and not its individual members, as is the case with Aboriginal or Native title. This empowers groups and puts incentives in place for them to organize themselves in order to be recognized by the state as possessing the appropriate legal and moral standing. Thus, group rights, like individual rights, may or may not promote cultural and societal heterogeneity. Group rights are compatible with the loose moral individualism of liberalism as long as those rights can be connected to promoting or protecting the legitimate interests of individuals in some way – interests they have *qua* individuals, but also those that can only be enjoyed jointly with others.

One way to think of the differences here is to distinguish between 'collective' and 'corporate' conceptions of group rights.[20] On the collective conception, a group right serves to protect or promote those interests that individuals have jointly with others and that are sufficient to impose duties upon others. The right is held by the group, but the interests that make the case for the right are the separate (although identical) interests of the group's members. The moral standing required for the rights claim is provided by the moral standing of the several individuals who make up the group. According to the corporate conception, on the other hand, the moral standing is ascribed to the group as such. The right is not held jointly by the individual members, but by the group as a unitary entity.

When we think of a group right in this corporate sense, the interests or values it serves are independent of the legitimate interests of the individuals who identify or associate with it. This can amount to saying that a culture or group is worth preserving, regardless of the desires, beliefs or interests of the individuals who identify with it. Sometimes the value of a nation or a people is defended in these terms. This worries many liberals – especially liberal egalitarians – because it seems to put the individual at the mercy of the group, even if membership of it is something she or he greatly values.

The complexity of Aboriginal rights comes with the overlay of a history of colonial domination. Indigenous polities find themselves in something of a double bind. The very legal and constitutional tools they reach for to protect themselves from political and cultural domination can be turned around to justify yet further colonial interference. And it's here that corporate and collective conceptions of rights can become intertwined and conflict in various ways.

Take, for example, the case of David Thomas, a member of the Coast Salish Nation, in British Columbia, Canada, who claimed he had been forcibly included in a 'Spirit Dancing' ceremony and sued the tribal government for assault, battery and false imprisonment (although a member of the Nation, he lived off-reserve).[21] This case tends to be interpreted very much through the lens of individual versus collective rights and the role of the common law in protecting individuals from harm. It might well be the legal case was correctly determined in Thomas's favour, and thus individual rights 'won'. However, in interpreting it so narrowly, we foreclose the sense in which there is a genuine conflict of laws here: do we have the appropriate institutional framework in place within which to address these kinds of conflicts? Political theorists tend to rush to their 'individualist' and 'collectivist' corners with these cases, without pausing to consider the complex contours of the matters at hand. The assumed individual/collective binary rests on static and homogenizing conceptions of Indigenous political and cultural practices and thus can sometimes unwittingly reinforce the very phenomena liberal critics believe they are challenging. As the Mohawk legal theorist Patricia Monture-Angus has argued, Aboriginal rights attempt to fuse together different normative and cultural traditions that need to be interpreted flexibly.[22] She and other Indigenous theorists point to the complex interdependency between individual and collective interests that form a crucial part of Aboriginal political theory and governance systems.

Thus, it's a gross over-simplification to say that Aboriginal rights are wholly 'communal' in nature. In some cases, within Aboriginal legal systems, individual rights are allocated and protected within a general communal right. In other cases, a communal interpretation of an Aboriginal right – especially when imposed by Western courts – can end up undermining the intricate balance between individual and community interests in Aboriginal law.[23] There is a general lesson here: the more we see these rights practices as existing within a living, breathing set of normative orders, the more we will encourage internal change that leads to cultural adaption and renewal. The less we do so, the more likely we are to encourage the telescoping and reification of demands.

For example, in the Canadian *Delgamuukw* case (1997), the Gitskan and Wet'suwet'en argued that the grounds for their rights claims lay in part in the *Adaawk* and *Kungax*: the complex oral histories and songs about their land and governance systems (as well as their physical representation on totem poles, blankets and crests), which are regularly performed and authenticated in ceremony. The court accepted that these oral histories should be given special weight in consideration of their claims.[24] They provided the normative contexts within which their rights could be elaborated, although these were limited, in this case, by the assumed pre-eminence of the Canadian constitution.

So where does this leave the defender of Aboriginal rights? Are they necessarily committed to the corporate conception of group rights? Consider another example, this time the right to self-determination. On the corporate conception, strictly construed, the right is owed to the group independently of the claims of individual members. The right is universal insofar as it is held by all tokens of the corporate type.[25] On the collective conception, the right is held jointly by the individuals in the group and is grounded in the interests they share in living in a self-determining political community. The right is universal insofar as the interests it serves are universal to all human beings. Thus, if Aboriginal rights include group rights in the collective as opposed to the corporate sense, then they are compatible with a family of liberal arguments about human rights (although there may still be deep disagreements over the kinds of interests at stake). The limits to any local customization of rights are established with reference to these collective interests.

It's clear that Indigenous peoples' rights are, at least along one important dimension, corporate rights in the stronger sense. One reason why has to do with imputing identity across time. The self-understanding of a group often takes on this corporate cast. A cultural group may claim a group right in order to ensure its survival into the future, as opposed to its mere security in the present, and thus is not entirely reducible to the current members of the group. This is a crucial element of policies designed to address historical injustice. Aboriginal property rights, which reside in the group as opposed to the individual members *per se* (although individuals can enjoy property interests within the collective title), require a corporate identity stretching back into the past and forward into the future. Indigenous groups are *peoples* without necessarily being states in waiting. This complicates the ontology within which much liberal political philosophy tends to operate. And it blurs familiar distinctions between civil and international society, as well as between cosmopolitanism and nationalism.

If Aboriginal rights are thus also corporate rights, whether flowing from Indigenous peoples' distinctive customs and laws, or their right to self-determination, does this mean they are based on essentially racial characteristics? Does it entail a form of biological or cultural essentialism that locks individuals into being treated as a member of a group whether they want to or not? The short answer is no – although there are always risks when institutionalizing group rights, collective or corporate, that we need to be alert to.

First of all, an Indigenous people is not a racial entity, but a political one: they are a polity. As a matter of fact, the membership rules of Indigenous polities prior to European settlement were not usually based on race at all and included sophisticated ways of incorporating new members from different nations and cultural backgrounds.[26] Thus, the grounds for treating Indigenous people differently, as a matter of justice, are not racial but normative. They share a collective and corporate right to self-determination on the basis of the interests that ground the right.

But if Indigenous peoples have political rights to self-determination, then how can they also have equal rights to participate in Australian or Canadian forms of government and citizenship? And don't group rights, whether corporate or collective, by providing protection for distinctive political and cultural identities, fly in the face of the kind of social solidarity required to realize the strong social and economic outcomes favoured by liberal egalitarians? Brian Barry, for example, argues that, 'to be a Pueblo Indian is to have a legal status that is equivalent to citizenship in a state' (albeit a 'sub-state with delegated powers').[27] The Pueblo cannot enjoy all of the constitutional guarantees of US citizenship except by giving up 'their special rights that flow from their Pueblo Indian citizenship'. Since aspects of Pueblo citizenship, such as a religious test determining the receipt of membership benefits, violate liberal principles of justice, in order to retain their 'special political status', the Pueblo 'should be required to observe the constraints on the use of political power that are imposed by liberal justice'.[28] For Barry, the Pueblo are perfectly free to form themselves into a 'religiously exclusive' community given liberal rights of freedom of association and religion, but they cannot combine religious exclusivity with the exercise of political power. In short, for him, Aboriginal rights undermine the equality and freedom of individuals at the heart of liberal conceptions of citizenship. They also threaten the civic unity required for broadly based social and economic programmes aimed at providing equal opportunity for all.

Barry presents a sharp normative challenge to defenders of Aboriginal rights: what is the fit between Aboriginal rights and citizenship rights? Again, the problem is not exclusively one of a clash between collective and individual rights. Both Aboriginal and citizenship rights are collective rights of a kind, since both define a particular

reference group within which a specific distribution of powers, liberties and immunities should
occur. Both are also culturally mediated in various
ways. Citizenship rights are not simply 'applied
liberalism, pure and simple', as Joseph Carens
puts it, but rather interpreted and applied through
distinctive legal and political institutions, 'with
their own norms, practices, interpretations and
modes of reasoning'.[29] The problem lies in the
differing content and scope of the interests to which
they refer.

Relying exclusively on the difference argument
to explain the nature of the fit between Aboriginal
rights and citizenship rights either ignores the
problem or ties the rights to a narrow set of
supposedly 'customary' practices. On the other
hand, simply asserting that Indigenous peoples
have already consented to being incorporated into
the state (as Barry does) begs the question. A better
justification has to be found.

Aboriginal rights relate to those particular interests
to do with territory, culture and self-government
that distinguish Indigenous peoples from other
kinds of groups in settler states like Australia,
Canada and the United States. These interests
are distinctive because they relate to the fact of
Aboriginal prior occupancy of and jurisdiction over

these territories, and to the challenges they face in maintaining their distinctive cultural practices and ways of life in the face of *ongoing* dispossession and political domination. The argument justifying the protection of these interests appeals to equality, but not only to the equal provision of the means to be self-determining. Other interests are also at stake. There are at least two.

First, Aboriginal rights promote the formal equality of peoples who were previously considered – from the perspective of both international and domestic law – as politically and culturally inferior and thus undeserving of equal consideration. Second, they promote equality in the substantive sense, as providing the tools for enabling Indigenous polities to address the social and economic disadvantages they continue to suffer from. Aboriginal rights are one way, but not the only way, of enabling Aboriginal people (in both the collective and corporate sense) to achieve their equal freedom.

Conclusion

There is a poignant moment in the Canadian *Delgamuukw* case when, after outlining the unique nature of Aboriginal rights, Justice Lamar adds that these should be respected, however, in a way that does not 'strain the Canadian legal and constitutional structure'.[30] But how is this possible? Without 'straining' existing legal and constitutional structures, liberal democratic states will never be able to arrive at just relations with Indigenous peoples.

What, then, *is* the best fit between Aboriginal rights, citizenship rights and human rights? First, as we have seen, it will be a complex fit, given the different sources of legal and normative 'orders' in play. What about the conflicts that might emerge between them? In considering these questions, I have made a plea to pay attention to the details of each case. But it also depends, as a matter of principle, on the extent to which those subject to the norms in question have been able to shape the institutions and practices shaping them. The more asymmetric the relations of power and the less scope for common deliberation about the consequences of the norms in question, the less secure the equal freedom of those subject to them. But this means negotiation and compromise on all sides.

Given the history of Indigenous peoples being subject to coercive assimilation by the state – often through the very language of 'equal citizenship rights' – it is unreasonable to expect them to see citizenship rights as providing, in themselves, an unproblematic basis for a 'common emancipatory project' (as Barry claims they do). Realizing justice as impartiality requires dealing with a legacy of state-enforced partiality first. Thus, the fit between Aboriginal rights and liberal rights will be an uneasy one, and closer to what political philosophers call a *modus vivendi*: a way and spirit of proceeding, despite the lack of a settled consensus on many of the key issues.

Needless to say, rights are not the be all and end all of politics. We have duties that are not reducible to claims about rights. And we can be unfree in ways that exceed our possession of rights. Moreover, if Aboriginal rights are unenforceable, or make no difference to the actual lives of Aboriginal peoples, then we may well have good reason to doubt them altogether. But there is nothing inherent to the language of rights that is incompatible with the ends Aboriginal peoples seek, at least as I understand them. The indeterminacy and yet wide acceptance of the language of rights mean that they can be (re)translated and put to work in new ways.

However, on its own, securing Aboriginal rights in liberal democracies provides only a limited solution to the challenge outlined in Chapter 1. If liberal rights are grounded in liberal conceptions of the person and political institutions, and Aboriginal rights in Aboriginal political theories and institutions, then how can the two be reconciled? We need to consider the overall political settlement within which liberal and Aboriginal forms of life can be situated – and one that does justice to the complex interdependencies between them. This is the focus of our final chapter.

4

Legitimacy and Justice

Introduction

In the Preface, I suggested that the 'Uluru Statement from the Heart' prefigures a new way of imagining just terms of political association between Indigenous peoples and liberal states. In previous chapters, we've explored how there is often a hidden premise about the inherent legitimacy of the liberal state that needs to be challenged in existing approaches to these issues. And so, in our final chapter, I want to try to be more explicit about what I suggested was so promising about the Uluru Statement. The call for an Indigenous 'Voice' to Parliament embedded in Australia's constitution, alongside a process of truth-telling and treaty-making, links backward- and forward-looking approaches to justice and ties them to a process of dialogue and engagement. How can we best capture the normative force of this vision?

Mutual Justification

The dominant liberal egalitarian approach to justice in Anglo-American political theory for half a century has been to try to identify a set of general principles that can guide the design and evaluation of our most important social and political institutions. The epitome of such an approach is found in the work of John Rawls. Can Rawlsian liberalism deal with the deep structures of inequality that have arisen in the wake of colonialism?

To do so we need a richer sense of the temporal dimensions of justice; how the past, present and future are interlinked in our thinking about what we owe to each other. But, second, we also need to focus on our 'practices of mutual justification'. What does this mean? The basic idea is simple enough: in making a claim, we are appealing to a set of reasons – in this case, to a standard of justice or right – that presupposes a certain picture of human agency and freedom. This picture includes the idea that we are the kind of creatures who give reasons and can respond to them. But it also trades on the deep sense that we can, at least in principle, form a common point of view about critical issues that concern us all. In politics this is vital: how should society be organized? Who should exercise power? How should the benefits and burdens of our cooperative activities be distributed?

The ideal of mutual justification is tied to a conception of persons conceived as fundamentally free and equal. To demand a justification for the power being exercised over you is to assert one's agency and freedom as a moral agent. It is to assert that might is not right and that any exercise of power must be accompanied by reasons – and not just *any* reasons ('it's my way or the highway!') – but ones that could form the basis of a genuinely common perspective. But what kinds of reasons would count as reasonable and why and for whom? It doesn't mean finding *The Reason*, so to speak, that compels my interlocutor to accept on pain of irrationality (or worse). But we do have to engage with each other's reasons – and crucially, in politics, the passions that underlie them – in the course of constructing a common view of our public institutions.

However, what philosophers call the 'uptake' of Indigenous peoples' claims in political discourse is deeply shaped by both historical and normative forces. To recover the hidden transcripts of

Indigenous peoples' political and legal struggles – listening closely to their voices – is to rediscover the political agency of their polities. And this means that we need to start much closer to the muddy ground of inter-societal (mis)understandings and negotiations.

Consider, then, two different ways of making sense of this idea of 'practices of mutual justification'. The first is a straightforward normative conception, whereby we seek the best justification – that which is true or valid – upon which the legitimacy or justice of a social and political order is grounded. The second is a more historical and empirical conception, whereby we pay close attention to the modes of justification that exist and how they came about, whether or not we think of them as ultimately true. Recall that, in Chapter 1, we encountered a bundle of beliefs about the nature of property, civil society, the state and the economy that held in place a vast array of colonial relations of power. Power can thus be exercised *through* our modes of justification as much as we demand justifications *of* the relations of power being exercised over us.[1] As a result, we need to pay as much attention to questions of legitimacy, as to questions of justice, and to examine how inequality can be reproduced and sustained through the very institutions intended to redress it.

How can political authority be legitimate where there is deep disagreement as a result of reasonable pluralism about the right and the good? And how can groups struggling to overcome enduring historical injustices ever come to affirm their membership of a political community in such a way that the political authority exercised over them is legitimate?

Recognition

One influential approach to addressing this challenge has been through the liberal 'politics of recognition', which we touched on briefly in Chapter 2. At the heart of this approach, drawing on the work of the German philosopher Georg Wilhelm Friedrich Hegel, is the claim that to become a self-conscious and self-determining agent, we need the recognition of other, similarly constituted beings.[2] The demand for recognition is thus a demand for mutual respect. Mis-recognition is a form of disrespect, an absence of mutual esteem, and can be harmful in at least two ways: either it undermines an individual's (or group's) capacity for self-development and freedom because they internalize the judgements of inferior social worth made by dominant groups; or it reinforces existing structural and material inequalities that impede their ability to participate equally in democratic institutions.[3] The first involves a psychological account of the role of recognition in political struggles. The second focuses on the way demands for recognition reflect deeper social, economic and political inequalities.

There have been two lines of critique of the politics of recognition. The first is that a focus on recognition often misconstrues the motives and aims of social and political actors engaged in political struggles. Recognition is certainly an important element of what is at stake in these contexts, but it is not the most important. In the most psychologically focused accounts, struggles over recognition become dominated by the quality of the individual's (or group's) sense of self-respect vis-à-vis their recognition by others. But this overemphasizes the need for mutual recognition as a condition for effective political agency. History suggests that individuals and groups form a sense of their own identity and self-worth both prior to and in the midst of often deeply unequal struggles for justice. After all, Hegel's slave ultimately gains his freedom only after turning *away* from his master and focusing on his own work.

The second line of critique is more specific. Who is doing the recognizing, and on what basis? The concern here is that casting the claims of Indigenous peoples as claims for recognition by the *state* is a trap. Indigenous political theorists have developed powerful versions of this critique, the essence of which is that colonialism makes mutual recognition impossible. Frantz Fanon, for example, argued that the colonial master is not dependent on the slave for securing his own self-consciousness, as Hegel thought, but rather needs his work (and, crucially, his land).[4] The colonial subject, in turn, subjects himself to a regime of recognition in which he internalizes the gaze of the colonizer, and thus attitudes, beliefs and desires that distort his self-understanding. The Kahnawà:ke anthropologist Audra Simpson argues, for example, that this means that the production of anthropological and political knowledge about Indigenous peoples ends up being wed 'elegantly, effortlessly and very cleanly' to the imperatives of the colonial project and the desire for territory.[5] This can result in divisive, overlapping and enduring injustices within Indigenous communities as well. Consider, for example, the situation facing Aboriginal women in Canada. Between 1876 and 1985, the Indian Act tied Indian 'status' to birth or marriage to a male Indian. Despite various legislative attempts to end this sex discrimination, the effects still linger. As the Dene political theorist Glen Coulthard well summarizes it, a racist and patriarchal Canadian Indian Act, combined with diminished territory and constrained rights of self-government, ends up generating yet more grounds for intervention in Aboriginal communities – which, in turn, generates new conflicts and divisions therein.[6]

What these critiques expose is the 'sting in the tail of recognition'.[7] To seek recognition is to seek to be valued by others, which invites a critical evaluation of the beliefs and practices of the person (or peoples) making the claim. The 'recognizer' thus exercises power over the 'recognizee' in having the capacity to grant such recognition in the first place. An alternative to the politics of recognition, according to Simpson and Coulthard, is thus one of *refusal*: to reject the game of recognition altogether.

Power and Justification

What critics of the liberal recognition game are drawing attention to is power. In refusing to play the recognition game, Indigenous peoples are disrupting the legitimacy of the liberal settler state.

Despite the focus on the justification and legitimacy in recent political theory, it's still not clear that liberal egalitarians really do put power at the heart of their analysis. If they did, it would shift the onus of justification from resting mainly with Indigenous polities to the settler state.

A frequent complaint about liberalism is that it lacks the resources to both analyse and attend to the role of structural power in politics. It's not just that the state and its agencies could (and do) interfere arbitrarily in the lives of Indigenous peoples, but that power is also exercised through the background conditions of society and through the apparently 'free' actions of those subject to it. The domination exercised directly through colonialist legal and institutional rules and policies is stabilized through accompanying narratives of political dysfunction and decline in Aboriginal communities. These shape the incentives, 'know-how' and even the claimed knowledge of what policy makers think should be done in these domains – sometimes, with the best of intentions. Even when those narratives are disrupted, the effects of the intersection of different relations of power can linger. For example, native title was finally recognized by the Australian High Court in 1992 in the famous *Mabo* decision, but the subsequent legal regime created to help recognize and protect it continues to struggle to deliver just outcomes for Indigenous land claimants. Can a different approach to liberal justification address the deep structural features of power and inequality?

A key turning point for liberal egalitarian theories of justice in the late twentieth century was indeed the development of Rawls's theory of 'justice as fairness'. His account builds on an idea of social cooperation dramatized via a stylized thought experiment, which he calls the 'original position'. He begins with the idea of society understood as a 'cooperative venture for mutual advantage' and in which the 'circumstances of justice' obtain.[8] The 'circumstances of justice' – an idea taken from the eighteenth-century Scottish philosopher David Hume – are the conditions required for a theory of justice to be required in the first place. They have two important elements: first, certain objective conditions, such as the coexistence of people 'on a definite geographical territory' and of roughly similar physical and mental powers; and, second, subjective conditions, namely that they have roughly similar needs and interests, such that mutually advantageous cooperation makes sense and is desirable.[9] Now imagine an ideal constitutional convention in which representatives of this society meet to decide how best to distribute the benefits (and burdens) of social cooperation, but without knowing particular facts about themselves, such as their age, gender, race, income or status. What kind of principles would they choose from behind this 'veil of ignorance', as Rawls calls it? He argues they would land on two: a principle of equal 'basic liberties' for all (which can't be traded off against other goods) and the 'difference principle', in which any social and economic inequalities that exist must be to the greatest benefit of the least advantaged members of society.[10] Moreover, to ensure what he calls the 'fair value' of the equal liberties for all, citizens must have a roughly equal chance of occupying public office and/or influencing public policy, regardless of their social or economic position. The fair value of liberty can become undermined if the rich are able to dominate political processes, and the worst off are trapped in poverty and powerlessness. A 'well-ordered' society is one in which the two principles of justice are accepted, and known to be accepted, and where each citizen takes responsibility for upholding the institutions formed in their wake.

In his book *Political Liberalism* (1996), Rawls worried that he had underestimated the consequences of the kind of moral and cultural pluralism found in liberal societies for his justificatory approach. Now justice as fairness needed to be conceived as a 'political conception', not a 'comprehensive' conception, which could be acceptable to citizens who otherwise held often radically different religious, philosophical and moral views.[11] He also thought that a liberal conception of justice required an accompanying liberal conception of legitimacy.

A state is legitimate, according to Rawls, when its coercive power is 'exercised in accordance with a constitution the essentials of which all citizens as free and equal may reasonably be expected to endorse in light of the principles acceptable to their common human reason'.[12] Moreover, the kind of consensus required for liberal legitimacy will need to reconcile principles of justice with what he called the 'settled' convictions of a particular society – 'provisional fixed points which any conception of justice must account for if it is to be reasonable for us', where 'us' refers to a particular group of citizens at a particular point in time. Public reasoning about justice has to hook into the (complex) public political culture of a given society in some way. That means that any political proposals (including for radical change) about the basic legal and political structure of a state must be grounded in reasons rooted in the public political culture of that society. 'Public reasons' are those reasons that *could be* shared in a deeply pluralistic society and which could form the basis of a common conception of justice.

Can Rawlsian public reason – and other broadly similar liberal approaches – serve as a standard for the kind of public justification required in a society still shaped by colonialism? Is this the appropriate starting point for thinking about the just accommodation of Indigenous peoples and liberal democracy? The short answer is no, but I don't think that means abandoning the concept of liberal legitimacy or public reason.

There are complex philosophical debates about the nature of justification that we don't have time to explore here. But at the heart of this approach, as we saw above, is a conception of normativity in which the validity of norms is grounded in a form of practical deliberation among equals. A norm is valid to the extent that it withstands a certain kind of justificatory procedure. There are, however, two significant challenges for this approach. The first is the limit of what justification can do. The source of normativity of the justificatory procedure itself is, more often than not, presumed. What grounds the normativity of justification? For some political philosophers, deeply influenced by Immanuel Kant, such normativity is implicit in the way we grasp the nature of practical reason itself. In other words, that normativity is tied to what it means to see oneself as a human moral agent in the first place, sharing a world with other moral agents and with whom I must coordinate my freedom. Rainer Forst, for example, argues that the normativity of justification – what he calls the 'right to justification' – is an 'autonomous' insight of practical reason; we grasp the other in light of the capacity to reason that each of us shares.[13]

Now, Forst's argument invites the charges of circularity and arbitrariness that the neo-Kantian tradition has long sought to avoid. I leave this critique aside here. The key point, for our purposes, is that the ground of normativity is modelled on conceptions of practical reason. But these are very much *our* practices of practical reason. Practical reasoning is a social practice as much as it is a practice of reasoning. It has a history. And that means that there is always the possibility that those practices have been shaped by arbitrary power which evades our existing conceptual and justificatory schemes. And this returns us to the question of power, as well as to the legacies of historical injustice. It's not that the project of reconstructing the ground of normativity is impossible. Rather, we need to address the challenge of redeeming normativity in light of the complex histories of our political communities. Normativity does indeed need to be grounded, but more in the sense of remaining close to where power is exercised and experienced. In seeking justice, we need to remain attuned to the particularized nature of injustice. Struggles for political justice, more often than not, start with an attempt by a marginal group to make particular injustices vivid in the face of majoritarian ignorance or intransigence.

Take, for example, the opening assumption upon which Rawls builds his entire conception of justice as fairness. The parties in the original position are supposed to already share a conception of society as a 'cooperative venture for mutual advantage'. As Charles Mills points out, this could only really be assumed for an audience that was completely ignorant of the consequences of slavery and settler colonialism in the founding of North America. As a result, for Mills, it is a 'ludicrously inapposite' starting point for constructing a political conception of justice for these contexts.[14]

And so we need to pluralize the liberal principle of legitimacy and its accompanying conception of public reason. We need to look for different sites of public reason – ones that are able to contest the self-understandings of the existing public political culture, as much as reinforce it – and find a way to connect them to a vision for a reimagined liberal democratic order.

A Constellation of Normative Orders

Our political communities are a plurality not only of cultures and peoples, but also of 'normative orders'.[15] We need to pay attention to the historical and political contexts in which these normative orders come into being and the interactions between them over time.

What do I mean by a 'normative order'? There is both a functionalist and prescriptive sense to the term as I intend it here. In the first, more basic sense, a normative order is any set of rules and shared expectations governing a particular social situation. But in the second, much richer sense, a normative order is a cluster of values, beliefs and legitimation 'narratives' (religious, cultural, moral, political and legal) that people appeal to in order to justify (and contest) the practices and institutions they are both subject to and help constitute. These normative orders are plural, because they are historically constituted, and dynamic, because they are undergoing change and modification through the actions of those subject to them.

What are the consequences of this picture of a plurality of normative orders for liberalism? First of all, instead of a liberal nation-state (even a multicultural one) being the political form within which Indigenous political communities are said to be subsumed, we need to conceive of a liberal political order as a constellation of normative orders that overlap and intersect in complex ways above and below the state. This means there are also a plurality of sites of public reason. Public reasons, you will recall, are those reasons we appeal to in order to justify the shape and function of the key legal, social and political institutions through which power is exercised. Indigenous activists and theorists, as we have seen, have presented powerful critiques of the existing ideas 'latent' in the public culture of contemporary liberal democracies. But they are also offering enticing new possibilities as well. Bruce Pascoe, for example, in his history of Aboriginal land practices in Australia, points to the deep knowledge and expertise bound up in Aboriginal conceptions of ecology and land custodianship that could help reorient Australian public culture in profound ways.[16] He is not only challenging predominant assumptions (and deep ignorance) about the history of Aboriginal peoples' agriculture by presenting evidence of their incredibly sophisticated farming and land management practices, but also pointing to new ways of conceiving of our relationship to the environment more generally.

But how is it possible to pluralize political authority and public reason and still have a genuine political community? In some cases, it isn't. If the differences are significant enough, there might be insufficient grounds for a shared sense of community. One thing the multicultural turn in political theory has taught us, as we saw in Chapter 2, is that assumptions about the cultural homogeneity of liberal states often overlooked the minority nations and peoples who had been incorporated into them. Unravelling and recognizing these features of a state might well entail reasonable grounds for secession by the unjustly incorporated group. But this doesn't follow in every case, and, interestingly, secession is rarely something appealed to by Indigenous polities. There are undoubtedly practical reasons for this. But another reason is because the structures of the modern state are not something Indigenous communities have necessarily sought to emulate. Sovereignty and self-government are still vital to their claims. However, it is as much a demand for the rethinking of liberal states as it is a demand to secede from them.

So how can the exercise of political power in settler political societies *become* legitimate? What is the 'source of normativity' for a genuinely postcolonial political legitimacy?

First of all, as I argued above, we need to distinguish between legitimacy and justice. The concepts are closely related – perhaps even interdependent – but not equivalent. Some argue that legitimacy is tightly aligned with justice, such that if the conditions required for citizens to exercise suitable 'justificatory power' are in place, just outcomes will follow. For others, like Rawls, we need an independent theory of justice, in addition to a liberal principle of legitimacy, in order to ensure that we arrive at just outcomes.

I don't propose to resolve this debate here. However, borrowing a distinction from Phillip Pettit, note two important aspects of legitimacy that we need to keep clear.[17] The first has to do with the quality of political relations between members of a political community. The second has to do with the outcomes the political system produces.

Starting with the second aspect, legitimacy is often linked to the outcomes and benefits individuals and groups enjoy as a result of the political process: the better the social outcomes for the larger number of citizens, the greater the legitimacy of the regime. However, it's clear that outcomes alone are not a sufficient condition for legitimacy, since they can be delivered through deeply problematic political processes. Recall the example of the Northern Territory 'Intervention' discussed in Chapter 3. The policy changes to welfare, land tenure and law enforcement were justified on the basis of an alarming rise in child sexual abuse, youth suicide, domestic violence and social dysfunction in various Aboriginal communities. These are desperately difficult matters. However, even if, for argument's sake, sending in the Australian army did, in fact, end up providing better conditions for the most vulnerable members of the community (and it's not clear that it did), there remain deep questions about the legitimacy of such an approach. Was there adequate consultation with those most adversely affected by dysfunction and the intended measures of the policy? Did they have the opportunity to respond to the recommendations of the original report? In other words, was there sufficient democratic control exercised by the people subject to the policies? At almost every level, the answer is no – understanding that, at the same time, there was (and remains) a desperate need to address severe social and economic disadvantage.

And so, legitimacy and justice can come apart. Social and economic goods can be distributed in illegitimate ways, including in ways that end up dominating the very people meant to benefit from them. But equally, the legitimacy of decision-making processes, and the institutions upon which they rest, can decay over time, particularly when the outcomes produced by these institutions are seen to be repeatedly unjust.

Thus, we need to attend to both the social and political dimensions of a conception of legitimacy. This has been a significant failing of many recent discussions of Indigenous peoples by egalitarian liberals. One reason why attempts at 'solving' entrenched Indigenous disadvantage fail is because of the lack of political (and moral) attention accorded to the importance of Indigenous normative orders in the construction of law and policy. In other words, there has been insufficient attention paid to the structural nature of the injustice underlying relations between settler states and Indigenous peoples. To lack adequate control over the laws, institutions and procedures to which you are subject (and which are unavoidable) is to lack the means to be free from domination.

Reconstructing Liberal Legitimacy

If liberal settler states are constellations of normative orders, then how can a plurality of normative authority be reconciled within a single political entity? How can these normative orders not only coexist in non-dominating ways, but also form the basis for a genuine political community? Could any liberal state (and the international order that surrounds it) be legitimate in these circumstances?

Deep disagreement is a fundamental condition of politics, or what Jeremy Waldron calls (borrowing from the Humean idea we explored above) the 'circumstances of politics'.[18] There are different ways of expressing this idea. For Rawls, 'reasonable disagreement' is a kind of normative fact about our democratic public culture that a liberal principle of legitimacy has to accommodate. This is not simply a form of political realism, but one of the consequences of people exercising their freedom. Nevertheless, we need to arrive at common decisions regarding our collective affairs.

The challenge for a distinctly liberal account of political legitimacy is thus to acknowledge the 'circumstances of politics' without giving up on the prospect of establishing legitimate political authority. Political decisions are complex and involve a large number of normative and empirical considerations. And this makes it difficult – even when there are normative facts that point in a particular direction – to construct a sufficiently justified collective belief about what is the correct action.

Consider two recent approaches to political legitimacy that focus on different dimensions of the legitimacy problem. In the first case, the focus is on trying to reconcile the competing 'wills' of members of a political community (the 'will-based approach'). In the second, the focus is on identifying the correct 'beliefs' that should guide the exercise of political authority (the 'belief-based approach').

According to the first dimension of the legitimacy problem, how do we accommodate the plurality and often conflicting claims about what ought to be done? How do we make political decisions on behalf of people with conflicting wills? Legitimate political decisions, on this view, adjudicate between the wills of citizens *in the right way*: as we've seen, for Rawls, this means deciding in accordance with a constitution 'the essentials of which all citizens as free and equal may reasonably be expected to endorse'.[19] For Pettit, on the other hand, citizens need to have 'equal control' over political decisions, which means essentially two things: first, they must have equal access to a 'system of popular influence over government' and be able to 'share equally in operating that system'; and, second, this 'system of popular influence' must impose a direction on government that all (who are subject to it) have equal reason to welcome.[20]

Thus, for both Rawls and Pettit, albeit for different reasons, each citizen must be able to endorse, in some reasonable way, the exercise of power that they are both subject to and help constitute. The challenge they both face, however, is how to justify this given the diversity of wills and beliefs about both the good and the right. There is also the problem of whether our existing electoral systems and institutions are capable of delivering genuine 'democratic control' in the first place.

According to the second dimension of the legitimacy problem, the challenge is to identify judgement-independent normative facts about what should be done. Political decisions, in other words, need to be responsive to valid claims about what *ought* to be done. The problem of political legitimacy is thus not only to adjudicate between conflicting wills, but also to identify the correct judgement about our political arrangements. Political decisions that entail genocide or the violation of human rights, for example, are illegitimate, not because they result in actions that fail to treat individuals with respect but because they are morally wrong. Validity does not stem from a process of adjudication between wills, but rather from the correct normative authority.

There is another aspect of the belief-based approach to political legitimacy that raises a further challenge. As Fabienne Peter has argued, according to this approach, the force of normative facts must somehow reach through to our will formation: it should help form our judgements about the validity and legitimacy of political decisions taken in our name.[21] The more successful the normative orientation that normative facts provide, the more significant the normative authority for determining the legitimacy of political decisions.

But here we return to the challenge outlined in Chapter 1. Normative justification always sits within history. The challenge for any conception of legitimacy – belief-based, will-based or realist – is to demonstrate how the acceptance of a justification for the exercise of power is not itself produced by the coercive power that needs to be justified in the first place. Does the colonial past and present of liberal settler states thus make the legitimacy of liberal democracy impossible? Are the institutions and practices of contemporary settler states so saturated by the legacy of colonialism that any claim to legitimacy – either now or in the future – is hopeless? The politics of 'refusal' articulated by Indigenous theorists such as Simpson and Coulthard trades on this powerful claim.

However, this way of characterizing the problem is perhaps too stark. The push and pull between the adjudication of wills and the attempt to establish normative authority *just is* the nature of political legitimacy. Tying justification to legitimacy means that political decisions must be justified *to* citizens: the reasons upon which legitimate political decision-making are based, in other words, are unavoidably agreement-dependent. This is so even if we believe there are agreement-independent normative facts that should guide political decision-making (i.e. that there are genuinely objective public reasons). The emphasis on 'justification-to' shifts the onus from the state to the citizen and the normative contexts within which they are situated.

The promise of this public justification approach outlined here is that it creates the conditions for the emergence of new forms of 'multi-personal' reasons that serve as the basis for the now more complex grounds of political legitimacy. Multi-personal reasons are reasons that can be endorsed from a range of different perspectives and that emerge from the bottom up – through ongoing, historically situated, multi-perspectival public reasoning – as opposed to 'top-down' state-based reasoning.

For this to occur, however, our modes of public reasoning must be open to counter-assertions and contestations of existing normative orders and authorities. Recall the challenge noted above when the very processes most in need of legitimation are rendered immune from contestation. For example, if we rule out, from the beginning, contesting the sources of political authority that inhere within Indigenous normative orders, then we are missing a key aspect of the ongoing injustice in our midst. What recent Indigenous activism has made clear is the extent to which we are often blind to these 'structures of domination'. And this can mean that the forms of mutual justification envisaged by liberal egalitarian theorists become practically impossible from the perspective of Indigenous peoples. Hence, political legitimacy needs to be pluralized to reveal the complex normative and constitutional structures of liberal settler states. However, and at the same time, we then need to develop the mechanisms and capacities for mediation, engagement and adjudication between these different orders, in order to (re)form the bases of new sources of legitimacy, and thus of new forms of political community.

Hope from Below ... and Above ...

There are two remarkable sources of hope that emerge at this stage. The first is the kind of proposal offered at Uluṟu. By providing a legal and political framework within which Indigenous peoples' voices can be heard on matters of deep concern to them, whilst at the same time engaging with the core political structures of the Australian state, it offers a distinctive opportunity for 're-founding' these relations. The promise is undoubtedly fleeting. Risks abound. But it offers to reset what seems currently fixed. Uluṟu offers new ground upon which practices of mutual justification can take hold, and for the emergence of new forms of public reasoning about what a just settlement between Indigenous and non-Indigenous peoples could be.

One thing it also does is refresh a rather tired debate about self-determination. It does so, in part, by tying the need for an Aboriginal voice in the constitution to the need to tell the truth about Australia's history. It makes vivid what is often lost in the arid texts of international law. But it also feeds off developments occurring at the international level as well, especially in the development and adoption of the Declaration of the Rights of Indigenous Peoples by the UN General Assembly in

2007. The Declaration seeks to move beyond the generic minority rights offered in other human rights instruments (such as Article 27 of the International Covenant on Civil and Political Rights), which left the question of the overarching legitimacy of the state unaddressed. It is an attempt by the international system – however grudgingly and imperfectly – to shuck off its imperial origins. But it is also a move, driven from below by Indigenous peoples, to pluralize the international system, just as they have sought to pluralize domestic ones. These two pincer movements seek to pluralize the state in profound ways. Thus, it is no surprise, depressingly, that Canada, Australia, New Zealand and the United States were among those states most reluctant to ratify the Declaration.

Consider, for example, the way self-determination has been conceived both in terms of intra-state and 'external' forms of autonomy, and yet also in relation to the language of human rights. It might seem to follow, given the history recounted above, that Indigenous peoples deserve to be accorded the same right to self-determination that was accorded to other groups during the previous decolonization era (which they were explicitly denied). But as we have seen, Indigenous political theorists point out that European notions of sovereignty and statehood are not necessarily the best match for their own understandings of self-rule.

However, there is a prior question of the extent to which self-determination is a claim demanded by justice and what follows in terms of the specific form and scope of such a right. The most prominent arguments for national self-determination have focused on the extent to which it secures the conditions for individual and collective autonomy. Enabling a group to protect its shared way of life is connected to how it helps individuals within the group to make sense of their freedom.[22] A related value is that it also enables a group to secure its collective freedom as non-domination: that is, the freedom not to be arbitrarily interfered with by other groups. But since we are always enmeshed in overlapping forms of interdependency – personal and collective, national and international – self-determination cannot mean freedom from interference *tout court*. The problem is *arbitrary* interference, not interference itself.

So, if the value of self-determination lies importantly in promoting freedom as non-domination, where does this leave the principle as applied to Indigenous peoples? They are owed a degree of political control over important aspects of their common life, but one that is also characterized by unavoidable interdependency and interconnectedness with others. Given the wide range of possible ways of interpreting what self-determination means and what is required to achieve it, it would be a mistake to talk about *the* right to self-determination: there will be many possibilities and variations thereof. If the language of self-determination is used too narrowly, without sensitivity to context, history and appropriateness of fit, it can end up telescoping demands and deepening conflict where flexibility and accommodation are required. Political self-determination is as much about the structure of one's relationships with others as it is about acting apart from them. What is striking – and ultimately hopeful – is how this more complex picture of relational autonomy and freedom is reflected in the construction of the Declaration, as it is in the Uluru Statement.

For example, the Declaration insists on a right to self-determination for Indigenous peoples, including the right to determine their own membership and the structure of their own institutions, but also that individual members have the right to obtain other citizenship as well (Article 32). Indigenous institutions are subject to internationally recognized human rights standards (Article 33) that apply equally to male and female 'indigenous individuals' (Article 43). The Declaration seeks to constrain states from encroaching on the capacity of Indigenous groups to exercise jurisdiction over their lands and waters, and, more generally, the right to 'maintain and strengthen' their distinct political, economic, social and cultural characteristics and legal systems (Article 4; also 26). However, the 'specific form' of this capacity is left ambiguous between 'self-determination', 'autonomy' and 'self-government' (Article 31).

The emergence of these movements from above and below the state also complicates a standard distinction in political theory between cosmopolitanism and nationalism. Indigenous peoples are often seen as defending a form of cultural nationalism and so fundamentally non-cosmopolitan in orientation. But this is too simplistic. Although there is no question that Indigenous polities are arguing for what Avery Kolers calls 'a right to place',[23] this sits alongside and within other sets of moral obligations, including to non-members outside (and within) their territories. And so, we need institutional mechanisms for enabling these different kinds of ethical and political considerations, across liberal and Indigenous normative orders, to be genuinely mediated, as opposed to being conceptually ruled out of court from the beginning.

For example, in 2017, the Dakota Access Pipeline protests saw the Standing Rock Sioux Tribe trying to uphold their treaty rights and block the US government from allowing an oil pipeline to run across their lands and near to rivers they depended on for a range of purposes. Given the existence of the treaty (violated but never voided), and the different ways in which the value of land, water and forests is conceptualized within Aboriginal normative orders more generally, there is a strong *prima facie* case for blocking the pipeline. This is a consequence of pluralizing public reasoning about justice. But if there were very different circumstances, such that denying access to land or water meant that non-members would suffer from severe harm, then more complex considerations would come into play. The special claims Indigenous peoples have to their territory would need to be weighed alongside other more general claims. However – and this is crucial – the history of colonial dispossession and how Indigenous peoples have repeatedly had their waterways and forests despoiled and been denied access to their traditional hunting and fishing grounds would also need to feature in public reasoning about these competing claims. The history of cosmopolitan political theory includes a legacy of justifying colonial dispossession, as much as it is also about egalitarian claims for access to resources.

Thus, we need institutional innovation in creating the conditions in which these complex and sometimes conflicting claims can be discussed and mediated. The constitutional and political fabric of liberal democracy does indeed need to be strained and stretched, despite what liberals might think. The Uluru Statement, as we've seen, proposes a mechanism for embedding just such a mechanism within the Australian Parliament and constitution. This would mean there was a deliberative body specifically constituted and designed to advise the Australian government on policies that had significant consequences for Australia's Indigenous peoples. There are other examples to draw from as well: the Sami Parliament in Norway, established in 1989; dedicated Maori electorates in the New Zealand Parliament (dating back to 1867); and the establishment of the public government of Nunavut, in Canada's north, in 1999. The constituent power of Indigenous polities needs to be harnessed by liberal democratic institutions as part of the process of re-founding them.

The Uluru Statement also calls for a genuine reckoning with Australia's history. This is a general requirement for all societies dealing with legacies of historical injustice. We must develop ways of deliberating about the past democratically. In South Africa, after the fall of apartheid, and in Eastern Europe, after the collapse of communism, 'Truth and Reconciliation' commissions became a means of tackling these issues – with varying degrees of success. Australia and Canada have embraced state-sponsored reconciliation processes for addressing the legacy of colonialism. However, these processes have tended to lack political credibility, especially from the perspective of Indigenous peoples. Whatever promise the idea of reconciliation might have possessed at some point has, I believe, been drained away in recent years. These particular reconciliation processes seemed designed to avoid the deepest challenges raised by the legacy of colonialism, rather than genuinely addressing them. And yet the need for institutional mechanisms for truth-telling about the past remain and there are lessons we can learn from these recent attempts. One of the most important is that the legitimacy question precedes and suffuses any search for 'reconciliation'. The Uluru Statement's call for *both* a constitutionalized Aboriginal 'Voice' and a careful, bottom-up truth-telling process makes this clear. Truth-telling has to inform any structural reform proposed to address the consequences of a history that is not yet past.

Acknowledging and grappling with the history of colonialism doesn't guarantee any particular political outcome. But doing so democratically involves developing a distinctive set of capacities: we need to try to see the world from the perspective of another, but then also commit to developing a shared set of practices and reasons for going on together. In Australia, for example, Noel Pearson has continually emphasized how one extraordinary benefit of a proper re-founding of the relationship between Aboriginal and non-Aboriginal Australia would be that the richness of what he calls 'ancient Australia' could become a source of a now pluralized but still overarching national identity.[24]

And so, ultimately, the arguments in this book reflect a conception of liberal democratic citizenship and political community that is grounded in an ethos of empathy formation as much as will formation. But the fact that empathy has to be *formed* through democratic practices is critical here. Empathy presupposes that you share a common ethical understanding of the situation of the other. But when it comes to Aboriginal and non-Aboriginal conceptions of the history of Australia, for example, and the legitimacy of some of its main institutions, it's clear that such a shared understanding remains something to be achieved, rather than assumed.

Thus, we should look for the glue of liberal democratic belonging not in pre-existing cultural or national traits, but rather in the way in which our democratic practices grapple with difference and disagreement. In other words, the kind of mutual reciprocity Rawls assumed as a starting point for his theory of justice has to instead be constructed over time. Belonging emerges from a practice of democratic citizenship, rather than being a precondition for it. A liberal democratic society is 'well-ordered', then, when I am committed to upholding those democratic institutions that help sustain and mediate just ways of accommodating and mediating between the social, cultural and normative differences we unavoidably live with. The drive of recent Indigenous movements to expose enduring injustices, but also to propose new ways of addressing them, is an extraordinary resource for free societies, as opposed to a threat to them.

But realizing this ideal won't be easy. The more we learn about the settlement of Australia or Canada, and the violence that attends to so much of that history, the greater the challenge to establish new modes of collective self-understanding and political legitimacy. And yet emergent movements like those associated with the Uluru Statement offer a powerful, possible way forward. In embracing the challenge presented in these new demands for justice, liberalism can begin not only to address deep historical wrongs, but also to develop a compelling vision for the future of liberal democracy.

Notes

Preface: Uluṟu

1 'Officially, there is no centre of Australia. This is because there are many complex but equally valid methods that can determine possible centres of a large, irregularly-shaped area – especially one that is curved by the earth's surface.' http://www.ga.gov.au/scientific-topics/national-location-information/dimensions/centre-of-australia-states-territories.
2 For an important discussion of the Regional Dialogue process see Appleby & Davis 2018.
3 Stanner 1968.

Chapter 1 The Challenge

1 Hobbes 1996: 486.

2 Wolfe 1999: 2. See the remarkable database of massacres of Aboriginal people in Australia between 1780 and 1930 at: https://c21ch.newcastle.edu.au/colonialmassacres/map.php.

3 See Tully 1993; Tuck 1999; Pitts 2005; Fitzmaurice 2014; Bell 2016.

4 Tully 1993.

5 Fitzmaurice 2014: 12–14, 59–170.

6 Williams 1990; Tully 1995; Slattery 2007.

7 Belmessous 2012.

8 *Mabo v. Queensland* 1992; *Mr A. Griffiths (deceased) and Lorraine Jones v. Northern Territory* 2019.

9 Anghie 2005.

10 Contrast Ypi 2013 and Stiltz 2015.

11 Bell 2016: 62–90.

12 Bell 2016: 90.

13 Levy 2014.

14 Levy 2014: 28.

15 Rawls 1996.

16 Okin 1999.

17 See Waldron 1992.

18 On 'enduring injustice', see Spinner-Halev 2012. On a diachronic approach, see Ivison 2002; Kolers 2009: 101–3.

19 Young 2011: 53–74.

20 Rawls 2005: 9–10.

21 Rawls 2001: 10.

22 Anderson 1999.

23 Young 1990: 38.

24 Pettit 2010; 2012; 2014.
25 Arendt 1973.
26 Forst 2012.
27 Compare Markell 2008 and Pettit 2012.
28 Schmitt 2007.

Chapter 2 Multiculturalism

 1 Kymlicka 1995; 2007b.
 2 Povinelli 2002.
 3 Kymlicka 2007b: 33–4.
 4 Young 1990; 2011.
 5 Schachar 2001; Eisenberg et al. 2014.
 6 Kymlicka 2007a: 34–5
 7 Taylor 1992.
 8 See *Mabo v. Queensland* 1992; *R v. Van der Peet* 1996
 9 Borrows 1992; *Report of the Royal Commission on Aboriginal Peoples* 1996. See also Turner 2006.
10 Anya 1996: 3.

Chapter 3 Rights

 1 See Monture-Angus 1999.
 2 Borrows 2010.
 3 Borrows 2010: 10.
 4 Slattery 2007.

5 As in *R v. Van der Peet* 1996; though modified in *R v. Delgamuukw* 1997.

6 Waldron 2003

7 Nozick 1974: ix.

8 Or all three – for a discussion see Ivison 2008.

9 Alfred 1999: 140; see also 57–8.

10 For a good overview see 'Rights', *Stanford Encyclopedia of Philosophy*: *https://plato.stanford. edu/entries/rights/*.

11 Patton 2009.

12 Slattery 1987; 2007; see also Fitzmaurice 2014.

13 Slattery 1987: 732.

14 Slattery 1987: 736–7.

15 Slattery 1987: 737–8.

16 In *Calder v. Attorney General of British Columbia*, the Supreme Court of Canada ruled, for the first time, that Aboriginal title existed as a matter of law in Canada, regardless of any grant or act of recognition by the Crown. Although the particular appeal was dismissed (three judges said the Nisga's title had been extinguished by laws pertaining to land enacted by British Columbia prior to Confederation; three judges said it had not; and one ruled the appeal out on the basis of a technicality), the underlying recognition of Aboriginal title represented a profound shift in Canadian jurisprudence. Similarly, in *Mabo v. Queensland (no. 2)*, the Australian High Court recognized, for the first time, that 'native title' had survived the introduction of English law to the

continent, and to the extent that it hadn't been validly extinguished by subsequent laws and acts.

17 See *R v. Sparrow* 1990.
18 *Report of the Royal Commission on Aboriginal Peoples* 1996: 675–95.
19 Tully 1995; 2008; Levy 2000.
20 Jones 1999.
21 *Thomas v. Norris* 1992.
22 Monture-Angus 1999; see also Metallic & Monture-Angus 2002.
23 Perhaps the most striking example of the distorting effects of this kind of imposition is the privileging of men's interests under the Canadian Indian Act (1875).
24 *R v. Delgamuukw* 1997: para. 98.
25 Jones 1999: 89.
26 Gover 2010.
27 Barry 2001: 189.
28 Barry 2001: 189.
29 Carens 2000: 192.
30 *R v. Delgamuukw* 1997: para. 82.

Chapter 4 Legitimacy and Justice

1 On these two ways of thinking of the relation between justification and power see Forst 2018.
2 Taylor 1992; Honneth 1996.

3 See Fraser & Honneth 2003.
4 Coulthard 2014.
5 Simpson 2014: 71.
6 Coulthard 2014: 100.
7 Webber 2014: 276.
8 Rawls 2001: 84.
9 Rawls 2001: 84, 101.
10 Rawls 2001: 42–50.
11 Rawls 1996: 11–15.
12 Rawls 1996: 137.
13 Forst 2013.
14 Mills 2009: 173.
15 I am grateful to Rainer Forst and his colleagues in the Cluster of Excellence on 'The Formation of Normative Orders' at Goethe University Frankfurt for helpful discussions of this idea.
16 Pascoe 2018.
17 Pettit 2012.
18 Waldron 1999: 152–5.
19 Rawls 1999: 137.
20 Pettit 2014: 12–13.
21 Peter 2009.
22 Kymlicka 1989; 1995; Miller 1995; 2007.
23 Kolers 2009.
24 Pearson 2014.

References

Alfred, T. 1999. *Peace, Power, Righteousness: An Indigenous Manifesto*. Don Mills, Ont.: Oxford University Press.

Anderson, E. 1999. 'What is the Point of Equality?' *Ethics* 109 (2): 287–337.

Anghie, A. 2005. *Imperialism, Sovereignty and the Making of International Law*. Cambridge: Cambridge University Press.

Anya, J. 1996. *Indigenous Peoples in International Law*. New York: Oxford University Press.

Appleby, G. & Davis, M. 2018. 'The Uluru Statement and the Promises of Truth'. *Australian Historical Studies* 49 (4): 501–9.

Arendt, H. 1973. *The Origins of Totalitarianism*. New York: Houghton Mifflin Harcourt.

Barry, B. 2001. *Culture and Equality: An Egalitarian Critique of Multiculturalism*. Cambridge: Polity.

References

Bell, D. 2016. *Reordering the World: Essays on Liberalism and Empire*. Princeton: Princeton University Press.

Belmessous, S. (ed.). 2012. *Native Claims: Indigenous Law against Empire, 1500–1920*. Oxford: Oxford University Press.

Borrows, J. 1992. 'A Genealogy of Law: Inherent Sovereignty and First Nations Self-Government'. *Osgoode Hall Law Journal* 30 (2): 291–353.

Borrows, J. 2010. *Canada's Indigenous Constitution*. Toronto: University of Toronto Press.

Carens, J. 2000. *Culture, Citizenship and Community: A Contextual Exploration of Justice as Evenhandedness*. Oxford: Oxford University Press.

Coulthard, G. 2014. *Red Skin, White Masks: Rejecting the Colonial Politics of Recognition*. Minneapolis: University of Minnesota Press.

Eisenberg, A., Webber, J., Coulthard, G. & Boisselle, A. (eds). 2014. *Recognition versus Self-Determination: The Dilemmas of Emancipatory Politics*. Vancouver: UBC Press.

Fitzmaurice, A. 2014. *Sovereignty, Property and Empire, 1500–2000*. Cambridge: Cambridge University Press.

Forst, R. 2012. *The Right to Justification: Elements of a Constructivist Theory of Justice*. New York. Columbia University Press.

Forst, R. 2013. *Justification and Critique: Towards a Critical Theory of Politics*. Cambridge: Polity.

Forst, R. 2018. 'Noumenal Power Revisited: A Reply to My Critics'. *Journal of Political Power* 11 (3): 294–321.

References

Fraser, N. & Honneth, A. 2003. *Redistribution or Recognition? A Political-Philosophical Exchange*, trans. J. Golb, J. Ingram & C. Wilke. London: Verso.

Gover, K. 2010. *Tribal Constitutionalism: States, Tribes and the Governance of Membership*. Oxford. Oxford University Press.

Hobbes, T. 1996. *Leviathan*, ed. R. Tuck. Cambridge: Cambridge University Press.

Honneth, A. 1996. *The Struggle for Recognition: The Moral Grammar of Social Conflicts*, trans. J. Anderson. Cambridge, Mass.: MIT Press.

Ivison, D. 2002. *Postcolonial Liberalism*. Cambridge: Cambridge University Press.

Ivison, D. 2008. *Rights*. London: Routledge.

Jones, P. 1999. 'Human Rights, Group Rights and Peoples' Rights'. *Human Rights Quarterly* 21 (1): 80–107.

Kolers, A. 2009. *Land, Conflict and Justice*. Cambridge: Cambridge University Press.

Kymlicka, W. 1989. *Liberalism, Community, Culture*. Oxford: Oxford University Press.

Kymlicka, W. 1995. *Multicultural Citizenship*. Oxford: Oxford University Press.

Kymlicka, W. 2007a. 'The Internationalization of Minority Rights'. *ICON: International Journal of Constitutional Law* 6 (1): 1–32.

Kymlicka, W. 2007b. *Multicultural Odysseys: Navigating the International Politics of Diversity*. Oxford: Oxford University Press.

References

Levy, J. 2000. *The Multiculturalism of Fear*. Oxford: Oxford University Press.

Levy, J. 2014. *Rationalism, Pluralism, and Freedom*. Oxford: Oxford University Press.

Markell, P. 2008. 'The Insufficiency of Non-Domination'. *Political Theory* 36 (1): 9–36.

Metallic, C. & Monture-Angus, P. 2002. 'Domestic Laws vs Aboriginal Visions: An Analysis of the Delgamuukw Decision'. *borderland e-journal* 1 (2): http://www.borderlands.net.au/vol1no2_2002/metallic_angus.html

Miller, D. 1995. *On Nationality*. Oxford: Oxford University Press.

Miller, D. 2007. *National Responsibility and Global Justice*. Oxford: Oxford University Press.

Mills, C. 2009. 'Rawls on Race/Race on Rawls'. *Southern Journal of Philosophy* 47 (1): 161–84.

Monture-Angus, P. 1999. 'Theoretical Foundations and Challenges of Aboriginal Rights', in *Journeying Forward: Dreaming First Nations Independence*. Halifax, NS: Fernwood Publishing.

Nozick, R. 1974. *Anarchy, State, and Utopia*. New York: Basic Books.

Okin, S.M. 1999. 'Is Multiculturalism Bad for Women?' in J. Cohen, M. Howard & M. C. Nussbaum (eds) *Is Multiculturalism Bad for Women?* Princeton: Princeton University Press.

Pascoe, B. 2018. *Dark Emu: Aboriginal Australia and the Birth of Agriculture*. Broome, WA: Magabala Books.

Patton, P. 2009. 'Rawls and the Legitimacy of the Australian Government'. *Australian Indigenous Law Review* 13 (2): 59–69.

Pearson, N. 2014. 'A Rightful Place: Race, Recognition and a More Complete Commonwealth'. *Quarterly Essay* 55 (September): 1–72.

Peter, F. 2009. *Democratic Legitimacy*. London: Routledge.

Pettit, P. 2010. 'Republican Law of Peoples'. *European Journal of Political Theory* 9 (1): 70–94.

Pettit, P. 2012. *On the People's Terms: A Republican Theory and Model of Democracy*. Cambridge: Cambridge University Press.

Pettit, P. 2014. *Just Freedom: A Moral Compass for a Complex World*. New York: W. W. Norton.

Pitts, J. 2005. *A Turn to Empire: The Rise of Imperial Liberalism in Britain and France*. Princeton: Princeton University Press.

Povinelli, E. 2002. *The Cunning of Recognition: Indigenous Alterities and the Making of Australian Multiculturalism*. Durham, NC: Duke University Press.

Rawls, J. 1996. *Political Liberalism: With a New Introduction and the 'Reply to Habermas'*. New York: Columbia University Press.

Rawls, J. 1999. *The Law of Peoples*. Cambridge, Mass.: Harvard University Press.

Rawls, J. 2001. *Justice as Fairness: A Restatement*, ed. E. Kelly. Cambridge, Mass.: Harvard University Press.

References

Rawls, J. 2005. *A Theory of Justice*. Cambridge, MA: Harvard University Press.

Report of the Royal Commission on Aboriginal Peoples. 1996. Ottawa: Government of Canada.

Schachar, A. 2001. *Multicultural Jurisdictions: Cultural Differences and Women's Rights*. Cambridge: Cambridge University Press.

Schmitt, K. 2007. *The Concept of the Political* (expanded edition), trans. G. Schwab. Chicago: University of Chicago Press.

Simpson, A. 2014. *Mohawk Interruptus: Political Life across the Borders of Settler States*. Durham, NC: Duke University Press.

Slattery, B. 1987. 'Understanding Aboriginal Rights'. *Canadian Bar Review* 66 (4): 727–83.

Slattery, B. 2007. 'The Generative Structure of Aboriginal Rights'. *Supreme Court Law Review* 38: 595–628.

Spinner-Halev, J. 2012. *Enduring Injustice*. Cambridge: Cambridge University Press.

Stanner, W.H. 1968. *After the Dreaming*. Crows Nest, NSW: ABC Enterprises.

Stiltz, A. 2015. 'Decolonization and Self-Determination'. *Social Philosophy and Policy* 32 (1): 1–24.

Taylor, C. 1992. 'The Politics of Recognition', in A. Gutmann (ed.) *Multiculturalism and the Politics of Recognition*. Princeton: Princeton University Press.

Tuck, R. 1999. *The Rights of War and Peace*. Oxford: Oxford University Press.

Tully, J. 1993. *An Approach to Political Philosophy:*

Locke in Contexts. Cambridge: Cambridge University Press.

Tully, J. 1995. *Strange Multiplicity: Constitutionalism in an Age of Diversity*. Cambridge: Cambridge University Press.

Tully, J. 2008. *Public Philosophy in a New Key: Imperialism and Civic Freedom*. Cambridge: Cambridge University Press.

Turner, D. 2006. *This is Not a Peace Pipe: Towards a Critical Indigenous Philosophy*. Toronto: University of Toronto Press.

Waldron, J. 1992. 'Superseding Historic Injustice'. *Ethics* 103 (1): 4–28.

Waldron, J. 1999. *Law and Disagreement*. Oxford: Oxford University Press.

Waldron, J. 2003. 'Indigeneity: First Peoples and Last Occupancy'. *New Zealand Journal of Public and International Law* 1 (1): 55–82.

Webber, J. 2014. 'The Generosity of Toleration', in A. Eisenberg, J. Webber, G. Coulthard & A. Boisselle (eds) *Recognition versus Self-Determination: The Dilemmas of Emancipatory Politics*. Vancouver: UBC Press.

Williams, R. 1990. *The American Indian in Western Legal Thought*. Oxford: Oxford University Press.

Wolfe, P. 1999. *Settler Colonialism and the Transformation of Anthropology*. London: Cassell

Young, I. M. 1990. *Justice and the Politics of Difference*. Princeton: Princeton University Press.

Young, I. M. 2011. *Responsibility for Justice.* Oxford: Oxford University Press.

Ypi, L. 2013. 'What's Wrong with Colonialism'. *Philosophy and Public Affairs* 41 (2): 158–91.

Cases

Calder v. Attorney General of British Columbia 1973. SCR 313.

Mabo and others v. Queensland (no. 2) 1992. 175 CLR 1.

Mr A. Griffiths (deceased) and Lorraine Jones on behalf of the Ngaliwurru and Nungali Peoples v. Northern Territory of Australia 2019. HCA 7.

R v. Delgamuukw 1997. 3 SCR 1010.

R v. Sparrow 1990. 1 SCR 1075.

R v. Van der Peet 1996. 2 SCR 507.

Thomas v. Norris 1992. 2 CNLR 139.